D1135677

HARRY THE POLIS
EVEN MORE LIES

. . .

HARRY MORRIS

First published 2006
by Black & White Publishing Ltd
99 Giles Street, Edinburgh, EH6 6BZ

ISBN 13: 978 1 84502 119 3
ISBN 10: 1 84502 119 1

Copyright © Harry Morris 2006

The right of Harry Morris to be identified as the author of this work has
been asserted by him in accordance with the Copyright, Designs and
Patents Act 1988.

All rights reserved. No part of this publication may be reproduced,
stored in a retrieval system, or transmitted in any form or by any means,
electronic, mechanical, photocopying, recording or otherwise, without
permission in writing from the Publisher.

A CIP catalogue record for this book is available from the British Library.

Typeset by RefineCatch Ltd, Bungay, Suffolk
Printed by Nørhaven Paperback A/S

• • •

For Samantha, Scott and Kimberly

• • •

Warrant Sale

• • •

It was a regular practice by neds who were wanted on an arrest warrant to call at the local police station on a Thursday evening or in the early hours of Friday morning and hand themselves in to the police, rather than pay their warrant fine.

They would then be conveyed by the police prison bus to HMP Barlinnie in the morning.

Then, due to overcrowding at the prison, they would inevitably be released on the Friday afternoon, after having been imprisoned for the morning only.

This was known to all neds as a 'quick turn-around'!

One particular night, Jimmy Walker, a well-known ned, called at the station and informed me he had an outstanding warrant and wanted to hand himself in, to be included in the morning prison bus run!

I checked the recent warrant list and, sure enough, his name was there – a warrant for a £390 fine or fourteen days' imprisonment.

Fed up with this regular action by the neds, I said very convincingly, 'Well, you're in luck Jimmy – your name is not here, son!'

'It must be there!' he said indignantly. 'The polis have been up at my hoose to lift me twice this week. The warrant's for £390!'

'Oh, right! I'm sorry, son, I didn't realise you were here to pay your £390 fine,' I replied facetiously.

'That will be right!' he said. 'If I'm up there first thing in the morning, I'll be oot by the afternoon – they don't keep ye in over the weekend. Nae room!'

'Well, son, I'd love to oblige and give you the jail, but I don't see a warrant with your name on it, so you'll just have to go away back home to your wife and weans!' I replied.

After he left the station, I arranged to have him arrested on the valid sheriff apprehension warrant in the early hours of the Saturday morning.

By arresting him at this particular time, he would be held in custody all weekend and wouldn't be going to Barlinnie until the following Monday morning.

On the Saturday morning, several hours after his successful arrest and prior to my going off duty, a Mrs James Walker called at my office and reluctantly handed over £390 cash for her husband Jimmy's warrant fine to effect his release from police custody.

She also stated, 'By the way, my Jimmy tried to haun himself in here oan Thursday, but the polis at the desk widnae let him and telt him tae go hame – ye didnae huv a warrant for him!!'

'Away and don't be silly, Mrs Walker!' I said. 'Jimmy's obviously been telling you porky pies to get himself a wee holiday away from you and the weans!' I then added for her to consider, 'I can personally assure you that the polis certainly don't ignore any accused person who is wanted on a sheriff's warrant. So I would suggest yer man is at it!'

David Hay Said He Will Pay

• • •

One of my favourite police motorcycle duties was escorting visiting football teams to Ibrox, Hampden and Celtic Park in Glasgow.

On one occasion it was Nottingham Forest who arrived to play Celtic in a European match!

I met with the Forest manager, Brian Clough, and introduced myself to him and vice versa.

Pleasantries completed, I then escorted the team through the city to Celtic Park for the game.

At the end of the game, I was outside the front door, waiting for Forest to reboard their coach, which would then take them to Glasgow Airport for their flight home.

Once all were aboard, I escorted them on my police motorcycle, with my blue lights flashing, as we sped along the M8 motorway.

Suddenly the coach driver began flashing his headlights and indicated he was pulling over on to the hard shoulder.

I stopped in front of the coach and was walking back to see what the problem was when the great man himself, Brian Clough, stepped off the team bus, approached me and asked if I knew where David Hay, the Celtic football manager, had his pub in Paisley.

I replied that I did and Brian asked me if it was possible to make a detour to it, en route to the airport, which I agreed to.

I carried on along the motorway, coming off at the exit that would take us along to David Hay's pub.

As we stopped outside the front door, Brian Clough got

off the team bus and went inside for a few moments, before returning and giving me the thumbs-up to continue on our journey!

On our arrival at the airport, Brian Clough came over and thanked me for my assistance, and I took the opportunity to ask him why he went into David Hay's pub.

'Simple, young man!' he replied in his illustrious voice. 'I ordered up drinks for everyone who was in the bar and told the staff to charge it to David Hay!!'

Question Time
. . .

In the song that goes, 'Is this the way to Amarillo? Every night I've been hugging my pillow,' what's all that about? Is he a mattress-muncher or what?

The Medical

· · ·

Feeling unwell for several days, I made an appointment to see my doctor and have a check-up.

After a thorough examination, he wrote me out a prescription and said, 'Right, Harry, I want you to take four tablets daily – one in the morning with a large glass of water, one at lunchtime with a large glass of water, one at teatime with another glass of water, and one last thing at night, washing it down with a large glass of water!'

I then asked him what exactly was wrong with me.

He looked me straight in the eye and said, 'Simple Harry – you're not drinking enough water!'

Which reminds me of the time I took my missus to the doctor's after she complained of chest pains.

As I sat waiting for her, the doctor came out to speak with me.

'What's up with her, Doctor?' I asked, concerned for her health.

'She has acute angina!' he replied.

To which I couldn't resist saying, 'She's got a cracking pair of tits as well, Doctor, but I'd rather we discussed what was up with her!'

Missing Person Now Home

...

About one o'clock one morning, a man called at the police station to report his fourteen-year-old son missing.

Apparently his son had gone off earlier in the evening to an open-air pop concert at Glasgow Green and had since failed to return home.

I told the father not to panic because, owing to the crowds attending the concert coupled with the volume of traffic on the roads, there had been a considerable amount of congestion and all the buses were running late.

However, to try and ease his obvious concern, I convinced him to go home and if his son had not arrived back by a certain time, I would initiate a missing person report and a search of the area.

I then issued him with the telephone number on which to contact me should his son return in the interim period.

At about 2.10 the same morning, I received a call informing me that the missing boy had finally arrived home safe and well.

While being given this good news, I suddenly recognised the voice of the female caller . . .

It was that of my long-suffering wife!

I had inadvertently given the missing boy's father my own private home number by mistake!!

My wife asked me if there were any more missing persons she should be concerned about.

Or could she please go back to her bed?!

Fooled You

· · ·

A good friend of mine in the police had a twin brother working in another part of Glasgow.

Both brothers, Stewart and Clyde, were well known and instantly recognisable. They were, as we say in Glasgow, 'as black as two in the morning'!

One particular night, Clyde was working in the Bridgeton area of Glasgow and responded to a call from an officer requiring urgent assistance with a serious disturbance involving several youths fighting.

He made his way at speed to the location and as he arrived the youths ran off in all directions.

The officers at the centre of the disturbance signalled for Clyde to chase the main instigator, pointing him out as he tried to make good his escape.

Clyde took to his heels and gave chase. Within a very short distance he had caught up with the youth and rugby-tackled him around the waist, forcing him to the ground.

The accused looked up at Clyde in total amazement, with his eyes wide open and shock written all over his face!

He continued to stare at Clyde in utter disbelief while being handcuffed.

So Clyde stared him right in the face and said, 'What's up with you, then? Have you never seen a Catholic before?'

Don't Panic, Mrs Mannering
· · ·

I attended a call from a young couple, who reported that they had not seen their elderly neighbour, Mrs Mannering, for some time.

She lived in the top-floor flat of a tenement on the main street of Rutherglen.

I asked the usual questions of them. 'When was she last seen?'

'Three days ago, when she returned from a visit to her son who lives in Morecambe!'

'Has she any relatives or friends up here?' I asked.

'No relatives, but she has a boyfriend who left to go home prior to you being called,' replied the neighbour.

'How old is he and did he gain entry to the house?' I enquired.

'He's in his seventies and he was at the door for ages, trying to get in, but there was no reply!' he answered.

I then began knocking loudly on her door but, as for her neighbours before me, there was no response from Mrs Mannering.

The young couple were beginning to think the worst for their elderly neighbour.

I informed them that the next step I would have to consider taking would be to force the front door and gain entry.

They were in agreement with this action.

The door was large and solid with a glass pane above it.

It had three locks fitted but only one was in use.

I then performed the statutory polis action – I opened the letter box and had a sniff!

Now, I'm not sure why we always do this, because most old people have a certain smell about them, you know what I mean? That smell of Abernethy biscuits and pish! Anyway, it looks good for the punters.

I began my demolition of the auld yin's door.

'Right, stand back and give me some room,' I said as I used all my force and my Doc Martens to boot the door lock.

I had to perform this action three or four times, before – crash! bang! wallop! – and the door burst open under my pressure.

As the lock gave way, the door swung open, then it crashed again as a safety chain broke, causing the door to strike a mirror on the wall behind the door, smashing it.

Then, before the door swung back to the closed position, the decorative glass pane above it shattered on impact.

I then pushed the door and the wood and glass debris aside.

As I entered the hallway, I was stunned and surprised to see the small frail figure of Mrs Mannering, with a look of fear etched across her face, standing staring back at me.

I had to react quickly to calm the situation, so I put my hands up, in a Basil Fawlty-type manner, and in Clive Dunn's *Dad's Army* fashion I shouted reassuringly at her, 'Don't panic, Mrs Mannering, don't panic! It's all right – it's just the police checking to see that you're safe and well!'

'Safe and well?' She looked like I had accelerated her sell-by date and she was about to drop down dead at my feet!

I then approached her, put my hands on her shoulders, turned her around and led her totally stunned and shocked tiny frail figure towards the living room, followed closely by the young couple who were extremely awkward and embarrassed by what had occurred owing to their obvious concern for their elderly neighbour.

I made my apologies and quickly passed the buck by saying I was acting on behalf of her young neighbours' advice and their genuine concern that she may have suffered a sudden illness or fallen over, injuring herself.

I then asked the neighbour to make her a cup of tea and, if possible, slip a couple of valium into it, as she appeared to be suffering from severe shock!

Then we had some tea, accompanied by some comforting hugs and cuddles from the young female neighbour (which I thoroughly enjoyed, to the annoyance of her husband — only kidding, it was Mrs Mannering she was cuddling). With some TLC, Mrs Mannering recovered from the terrifying surprise of her unexpected gatecrashers.

TLC in this scenario referring to 'The Loony Cop'!

I left in the knowledge that the young neighbour would replace the glass and effect the repair of the demolished door and locks.

This being the case, I wished them all the best.

They thanked me for my professionalism and I made a hasty retreat!

While Mrs Mannering was still breathing on her own, without any assistance.

However! Please don't let this story put you off

contacting the police if you haven't seen your elderly neighbour for a few days.

Remember – we are here to assist the public! Just don't call me!

Rabbie Burns? Naw, Sidney!
. . .

I was escorting an old man to a hospital for mental health patients.

While I was talking to him, he informed me his name was Sidney and he was a poet.

On arrival at the hospital he handed me a piece of notepaper as he was getting out.

The following is what he had written:

There was an old man called Sidney
Who lost a dawd off his kidney.
He prayed to the Lord to give him it back.
He said that he would but he didnae!
Sidney!

Road Accident Excuses
. . .

'I approached the intersection and a sign suddenly appeared in a place where no stop sign had ever appeared before. I was unable to stop in time to avoid the accident.'

The Legless OAP

...

My partner and I called into his local pub after our shift for a few beers before going home.

Afterwards, we were about to leave when the barman asked if we could do him a favour by taking an elderly man along the road to his nearby house at number 12.

We agreed to his request and went over to where the old man was sitting sleeping, the worse for drink.

As we picked him up, the telephone in the bar rang.

'That'll be his wife!' said the barman. 'I'll let her know you're on your way.'

While taking him out, he was dragging his feet and mumbling to us and I said, 'C'mon, auld yin, let's see you walking. Use your legs!'

But my request fell on deaf ears. He was totally pissed!

All the way out to my car, I berated him about his condition.

'What a state to get yourself into, you auld bugger. I've heard of people getting legless but this is ridiculous. You can't even stand up! Ye better no' be sick in my car!'

The old man tried to answer back but his speech was slurred.

We placed him in the car and drove him the short journey to where he stayed.

As we were helping him out, an elderly lady appeared at the front door, holding it open.

She directed us inside to a bedroom, where we laid him flat out on the bed.

The old lady thanked us as we left to get back into our car.

We were about to drive off when we saw the old lady at the window, waving frantically.

I got out the car and ran inside.

'What's wrong, hen?' I asked, showing concern for her husband.

To which she replied, 'You've forgotten to pick up his Zimmer frame from the pub and he can't walk without it!'

A Word in Your Ear
• • •

A police sergeant, Ray McVicar, was having a running dispute with a civilian telephonist, Jesse Stewart.

One day in particular she was deliberately diverting his calls to other extensions in the office and generally mucking him about.

Finally he had had enough and a confrontation was inevitable.

He went to the telephonists' room and said, 'Excuse me, Jesse, can I have a word?'

To which Jesse replied, without turning around to face him, 'You can have two and the second one's off.'

Making a Big Impression

...

Prior to joining the police, I worked in a microwave oven factory.

It was good in as much as you could do your eight-hour shift in only twelve minutes.

Mind you, if you were working on the 850-watts, you could finish even quicker.

I remember going for my first interview to join the police.

I said to my mother, 'Mum, I'm joining the Glasgow police.'

She replied, 'I don't believe my ears!'

I responded, 'It's a bit late to start thinking about your looks!'

All dressed up, I arrived at Oxford Street Police Training College.

The inspector was very impressed with my appearance, although he didn't think my white spats went with my short trousers!

I was instructed to go up to the gymnasium so they could check my fitness levels.

As I was going in, a sergeant was coming out carrying a racquet.

On seeing me, he put his hand out and said, 'I'm a little stiff from badminton!'

So I said, 'Pleased to meet you – I'm a fat bastard from Glasgow.'

While at the college, I was asked by an instructor if I wanted to purchase a ticket for the Chief Constable's Ball.

I replied in all innocence, 'I don't dance!'
He said, 'It's not a dance, it's a raffle!'
Ah, well, the old ones are the best!!

Daddy! Guess What?
• • •

My eldest daughter Samantha arrived home late the other night, after being out with her friends in my new car, and said, 'Dad! I have good news and I have bad news!'

'Don't you tell me any bad news!' I said. 'I only want to hear good news!'

'OK!' she replied. 'The air bags are working in the new car!'

A Midge's Dick

. . .

Tommy Payne and I dealt with a serious assault, whereby a young man was struck on the face with a knife.

We obtained statements from witnesses, including the hospital doctor who treated the victim's wound.

After a short time we arrested the person responsible for this vicious assault.

Months later I received a citation to attend the Sheriff Court as a witness for the prosecution.

Tommy called me and said he would attend the registry in the police station and obtain the necessary witness statements required for the court case.

At the court, prior to the case being called, I was reading over my statement to familiarise myself with the incident reported.

'What did the doctor at the hospital say about the victim's injuries?' I asked Tommy, while thumbing my way through the witness statements.

Tommy replied casually, 'The doc stated he was a midge's dick away from losing his eye!'

'A midge's dick? A midge's dick?' I repeated.

I then began to flick my way through the hospital doctor's expert medical statement.

'That must be a new medical term for it,' I said to Tommy. 'But I doubt very much if it's in the *British Medical Journal*.'

Sudden Death

• • •

As a new recruit to the police force, I would spend one day per week at the police training school where I would take part in a weekly 'home study' course.

I would be given a questionnaire outlining a scenario, and the objective would be to detail what police action and procedure you would take to resolve the situation.

One nightshift, I was reading through my home study paper, writing down full details of everything I could think of to perform.

Roy Leslie, who was quite a laid-back character, was my senior partner for the entire five-week nightshift and he asked me what I was doing.

I told him it was my home study report for the training school sergeant, which I had to submit the following day.

'Well, just remember, Harry son,' he said, 'don't ever be stuck for an answer. I'm here to help you so you can ask me anything.'

With Roy's offer of advice and his obvious experience, I said, 'Well, if I read over the action I'd take, with regards to an incident involving a gas leak, will you tell me if you think it's all right and make sure I've not forgotten anything that might be obvious for my report?'

'Definitely, Harry, just you go for it. I'm all ears!' replied Roy.

'Right, then!' I said, excited by his offer of help. 'The scenario is, you are passing a tenement and you detect a strong smell of gas emanating from within. Detail in full what action, if any, you would you take.'

'OK,' said Roy. 'Let's hear it!'

'Right, first, I would evacuate all the residents of the tenement building, as quickly and quietly as possible so as not to create a panic situation. Next, I would contact all emergency services, such as the gas and electricity, to have them switch off all appliances at the supply source. I would contact the fire brigade and the police to help with the evacuation of all the residents and have the police traffic control set up all vehicular diversions, along with the roads department. Then I would have emergency ambulance crews attend and assist in conveying to hospital any elderly persons who might be suffering any ill-health problems. I'd request the social services to attend and assist with temporary housing for the evacuated residents and give serious consideration to evacuating the adjoining tenement building on either side, just as a precaution.'

Having detailed the actions I would take to deal with all aspects of the situation, I said, 'What do you think about that, Roy? Is that the action you would take?'

Roy thought for a moment, lit up a cigarette then said, 'You're creating too much work for yourself, Harry, and you have involved far too many people in your scenario. Your witness list will resemble a BT telephone book. You'll have more chapters in your report than *Gone wi' the Wind*! You've got to try and keep things tight and simple in this job.

'Now here's my advice of how to deal with it efficiently! Right, the scenario – you smell gas up a tenement close. What do you do? Simple! You stand to one side of the close mouth, you light up a cigarette and then throw the lit match up the close – Boom!!! – the whole building blows up and everybody up the tenement close is totally wiped out! Completely pan bread! Then all you have is a simple Sudden Death Report form to fill out. Now, is that not a helluva lot less writing and a much easier way to deal with it than your idea?'

Blowing Your Own Trumpet

• • •

Several years ago, the Strathclyde Police Federation held a meeting with their counterparts of the Royal Ulster Constabulary, whereby the Irish officers treated the Strathclyde members to a slap-up dinner followed by a cabaret.

As they took their seats along the front row, Willie Irwin, who was the Strathclyde Federation secretary and had a fairly big nose coupled with a dashing Clark Gable lookalike moustache, positioned himself at the centre of the delegation.

Halfway through the show it was the turn of an Irish comedian to perform for them.

After a few jokes, the comedian looked at Willie in the front row and with a puzzled expression he said, 'Here, sir, you must be really proud of that nose you have there. I mean, why else would you want to underline it?'

That's a Bargain

· · ·

All dressed up in our casual civvies for a boys' night out, we decided to meet up in a local pub in our working area.

As we all sat around with numerous drinks in front of us and taking up several tables, the door opened and in came a typical Glesca punter, dressed in a black jerkin and black baseball cap, carrying a large, fully laden sports bag.

He walked up to our table and, bending down to open up his sports bag to display the contents, he pulled out some colourful T-shirts and said, 'Right, guys, if you're interested in a bargain, I'm prepared to let you have these for a steal!' He then jokingly added, 'Mind you, if the polis stop you, I'll deny I sold them to you!'

He then paused and looked around at us all staring straight at him then, shaking his head, he threw his arms out from his sides and said, 'What?'

The reaction from us all was as one, as we produced our police warrant identification cards in unison at our cocky little Del Boy Trotter.

As he focused on them, first there was shock, then there was horror, then there was a loud, 'Whoosh! Bang! Wallop!'

He was off like an Exocet missile, leaving the bar doors swinging in his wake and some tasty designer T-shirts in his bag! It wasn't long before he was apprehended, with the many witnesses present all too keen to accept a recall to duty and the guaranteed overtime payment that goes with it.

To crown it all off, his real name was Roddy Bain, full name Rodney!

What a plonker!

Restaurant Tour

• • •

Harry Copeland and I were police recruits together and were both attending the training college in Oxford Street, Glasgow.

One lunchtime Harry asked me if I would accompany him to the city centre while he bought a new folder for his college notes.

He also added that he would buy me lunch.

I agreed and, in our brand new uniforms, just out the box, we walked across the old suspension bridge over the Clyde and into the centre of town.

The skip of Harry's police hat resembled a homing pigeon's landing board!

We entered the stationery shop, where Harry bought his folder, and afterwards decided we both should go into a nearby Wimpy for a burger lunch. (No McDonald's in those days!)

As we entered and sat at a table in the front of the café in full view of the public and ordered from the menu, an assistant came over to us and said, 'Excuse me, would you like to come to the back shop and sit?'

We looked at each other and Harry enquired for us both, rather naively, 'Why?'

'That's where you always go and you'll get peace to eat it!' she replied.

We looked at each other and nodded in agreement.

'OK,' we said and followed her to the back shop, where a table was set out with our order of burgers and coffees!

We sat down and ate our meal and, as we made to leave, Harry asked for the bill to pay.

The manager looked at us as if we were daft and said, 'Not at all, lads. Thank you for coming in!'

Quite excited by this reaction towards us, we walked over to the pancake place directly opposite, where we discovered they adopted the same attitude towards us.

Afterwards we returned to the training school, impressed by the response we received on our first day out in uniform and desperate to tell the others.

During the afternoon, the class was interrupted with the intervention of the training school inspector, who had received a complaint from the local beat cops regarding two young police officers having been observed operating in their area.

Harry and I responded with due responsibility for our actions – by sliding uneasily down our seats and, along with the other students, we totally denied it.

As for the real beat cops?

No doubt they had to pay full price for their lunch that day.

We Live in a Concrete Jungle

...

'Tank', the likeable rogue who was the scrap metal man around the Bridgeton area, decided to take the wife and weans away for a day to Blair Drummond Safari Park.

All packed up with the sandwiches and bottles of Irn Bru, they were off to spend a day with nature and wildlife!

After stopping at several interesting spots on their way around and enjoying the view of the various animals on show, they stopped to see if they could spot any lions!

'Oh, look, Dad – there's a sign! We're in the "Dangeroos" area!'

'Let's see if we can spot Flipper hopping aboot mad!' said one of the other kids.

'That's no' "Dangeroos", son,' replied Tank. 'It's a sign saying, "Beware, *dangerous* area"! Anyway, you'd have a hard job spotting Flipper, 'cause he was a dolphin, ya wee tottie!'

'Oh, so he wiz! Ah meant to say Zippy.'

'Ye mean Skippy!' said his mum.

They sat in their van for quite a while, waiting patiently to hopefully catch a glimpse of a lion, but to no avail.

Getting slightly frustrated and restless, the kids decided to open the side door of the van for some fresh air and slip outside to stretch their legs and maybe even just have the obligatory pee against the side of the van.

No sooner had the kids all got out than all hell broke loose.

Loud sirens and wailing horns went off at a high pitch, terrifying the poor weans, who all panicked and promptly

EVEN MORE LIES ••• 23

jumped back into the van, as two Land Rovers with safari park rangers, all kitted out, came screeching to a halt alongside their van.

As the rangers got out to check everything was all right with them, the weans, terrified by the alarms and the appearance of the park rangers, blurted out in a true Glaswegian fashion, all together, 'We never touched yer fuckin' lions!!'

Little Arrows on Your Suit
. . .

I once had the privilege of meeting and providing a motor-cycle escort for Sir Elton John to his concert at the SECC, Glasgow.

I was instructed to go to the Holiday Inn and meet him, along with his manager, John Reid, to sort out the arrangements.

I met with them and found Elton to be an extremely friendly and hospitable person.

'I'll wear something special for you tonight, Harry!' he said as I left the hotel.

I returned later to escort him and he came walking out from the hotel wearing a convict's uniform and hat, with the little arrows all over it!

As he approached me he then threw his hands up and said, 'Howzat?'

Saved Yer Life

...

The police attended a report of a suicide in a mental health home. The following is an account of what took place.

Two doctors were watching some patients exercising in the hospital swimming pool when the now deceased male jumped in at the deep end and sank to the bottom.

On seeing a fellow patient in difficulty, Thomas dived into the bottom of the pool and put his arms around the man's waist and pulled him up to the surface, where he helped him out on to the side of the pool.

One of the doctors watching thought this was a heroic thing for Thomas to do, and it was certainly a show of true concern for the life of another being.

It was his expert opinion that this act was not the act of someone who ought to be regarded as mentally insane.

With this in mind, the doctor reopened Thomas's case files.

Several days later, the doctor called at Thomas's room and said, 'Thomas, I have good news and bad news! The good news is that after seeing you risk your own life to rescue a fellow patient in extreme distress and danger to his life and your own, I have re-evaluated your case and now find you sane enough to go home! However, the bad news is that the patient you rescued went back to his room and unfortunately hanged himself with his dressing-gown belt!'

To which Thomas boldly replied, 'No, he didn't – I hung him up there to dry!'

Heart Attack? My Arse!

. . .

While I was at Tulliallan Police Training College, the student always sitting next to me in alphabetical order was big John Montgomery.

John was a very clever, educated student but slightly naive at times and a bit of a daydreamer.

Once a week at the college, the last class of the day would entail a lecture from a local man on first aid.

Nice wee man that he was, he had all these 'funny' lines he would introduce during his lesson and they were a bit dated, obviously having been an integral part of his lecture for many a year.

Suffice to say he was about as funny as a heart attack. (That's a medical term.)

One day, during his lecture, big John was slightly bored and unable to retain his concentration. As a result he drifted off into one of his deep daydreams.

The wee man was describing the position of the heart in the human body and how it was protected by what he described as a 'cage' immediately behind the bone called the sternum or breastbone!

At this, he spotted John sitting with a vacant look on his face, yawning away, and said, 'You there, with your mouth opened catching flies!'

At which point I nudged big John.

'What is it called?' he asked John.

John stood up and didn't have a clue what he was on about. He then looked at me for some prompting.

Being the obliging person I am, I whispered to John, 'Your rectum!'

John then blurted out loudly and confidently, 'Your rectum!'

At which point the entire class of students burst out laughing and the wee man said, 'Watch how you sit back down – I don't fancy giving you resuscitating heart massage!'

It's How You Say It

. . .

During the mad cow disease outbreak, I was explaining to my children that, for the time being, we would not be eating any more beef.

My seven-year-old daughter Kimmy was standing with a puzzled look on her face and said, 'Does that mean we'll all have to become virgins?'

I later explained the word was 'vegans'.

Question Time

. . .

In the Australian song that goes, 'Tie me kangaroo down, sport, tie me kangaroo down', why do they want to tie the kangaroo down . . . and what is the sport?

The Sixth Sense
. . .

The other night, to pass the time, my partner was showing me some old videos of her family which had been taken at different functions.

'That's my Aunt Isabel and my Uncle Robert. He died two years ago with a heart attack and she died not long after. Oh, and her running up the path, that's my Aunt Ella. She's been widowed for years. My Uncle Sam died while they were on holiday in Turkey. Food poisoning, they reckon.'

'With names like Sam an' Ella, I'm not surprised!' I responded.

'There's my Aunt Ina. She was the one who died in her sleep and you ran my mother over to her funeral at Daldowie Cemetery, remember? They spelt her name wrong on the headstone and put "Ian" instead of "Ina"! That's Agnes who my mum goes to the bingo with, and her man George. He suffered a massive heart attack. Poor Agnes came in from the bingo and thought he was sleeping in the chair. What a shock she got when she tried to waken him for his bed an hour later! Oh, and that's Mary and Tommy who stayed across the road from my mum and dad. They both died of cancer within a month of each other!'

After five minutes of this I had to ask her to switch it off, I was getting so depressed. I felt like Haley Joel Osment in the *The Sixth Sense*.

'*I see dead people!*'

Cheers Clarky

• • •

Another time during my training at Tulliallan Police College, Jimmy Clark and I were always in trouble and regularly given punishment details. Not for anything bad, I might add.

One particular punishment was for parking in the wrong area. As junior division recruits, we were detailed to help out at the final qualifying-night party being held for the senior division following their final passing-out parade.

This entailed Jimmy and I helping to serve them with their meal then, when they had finished eating, we would be required to clear the tables and collect all the crockery and cutlery for washing.

During this part of the evening, all the senior division had entered the Crush Hall, where they had a bar and a disco set up.

Once we had finished clearing up, Jimmy and I were about to leave when we were instructed to attend at the Crush Hall and help the bar staff collect the empty glasses!

Under protest we both attended and, as we entered, the party was winding down, although there was a good majority of them still on the floor dancing.

The tables were laden with drink as we went about, weaving our way in and out with our trays, collecting the empty glasses.

At one table there were a lot of full glasses so Jimmy and I decided to clear up quicker by helping to empty them.

I had the whisky and Jimmy had the vodka.

Every time a table got up to dance, Jimmy and I would move in like the man in black in the Milk Tray advert and, during their absence, we would help relieve them of their hangover by draining their glass for them!

It turned out to be one of the best punishment details we were ever on.

Hic! Cheers, Clarky! Hic!

Seen from a Satellite
• • •

During a court case at the High Court in Glasgow, a witness was giving evidence and telling the court of having seen the accused run off after the alleged incident.

The advocate depute asked the witness if he could identify the accused.

'Yes,' replied the witness. 'That's him there!'

At that he pointed to the accused male in the dock.

'What was he wearing on the night?' asked the depute.

'He was wearing a very distinctive Celtic football top!' he answered.

The judge then interrupted the depute and asked the witness, 'Tell me, was it that hideously bright luminous yellow one that can be seen from a satellite?'

'No, m'lord!' replied the witness. 'It was that hideously bright one with the stripes!'

That's Nuts

· · ·

A guy walked into a pub and ordered up a pint of beer.

After the barman poured his pint, he placed a tub of peanuts in front of him.

The guy was about to help himself to some nuts when a voice said, 'May I just say, sir, you are an extremely handsome man!'

He looked around but could see no one near him. He shrugged his shoulders and was about to help himself to the nuts when the same voice repeated, 'You're an extremely handsome man!'

As he looked down, the peanuts said, 'Yes, it's us talking, sir!'

'Crikey!' he thought to himself. 'I need a cigarette.' And he slipped off his stool at the bar and walked over to the cigarette machine.

As he was about to insert his money, the cigarette machine said, 'Here, ya ugly bastard, get lost. Go on, bugger off! Ye're getting nae fags oot o' me. Now beat it, ya big fanny!'

He couldn't comprehend what he was hearing and returned to his seat at the bar. He was completely dumfounded and confided in the barman, telling him of his experience with the peanuts and the cigarette machine.

The barman apologised immediately and said, 'I know, mate. All I can say is the peanuts are complimentary and the cigarette machine is out of order!'

Video Evidence

· · ·

A police social club was suffering regular thefts of bottles of spirits from the bar.

This was apparently occurring during the night, when the social club was closed.

The police were the only other personnel in possession of keys to the secured bar area.

Unbeknown to all shifts, a video camera was installed to record when the bar doors were opened and entry gained.

Two weeks later an inspector was taking up his dayshift duty when he was summoned to attend at the divisional superintendent's office.

As he entered the room, the superintendent instructed him to take a seat and view with him a video recording.

The video started up with a view of the bar area and a blonde uniformed policewoman entering the room closely followed by the inspector himself.

They began to kiss and cuddle, then the temperature was raised as they began to fondle, grope and remove each other's clothing, before participating in the dirty stuff on top of the pool table.

(No, it's not a Jackie Collins novel!)

When finished, they kissed, before getting dressed and leaving the room.

As the video ended, the superintendent turned around to face the inspector and said, 'Well, Inspector, have you anything you would like to say about what you have just seen?'

The inspector sat for a moment, digesting the contents

of the video, then said to the superintendent, 'With all due respect, sir, I think that video confirms that the police-woman and I had no involvement with the theft of any bottles of spirits!'

Silent Mugging

. . .

A funny thing happened to me one morning while en route to my work. Come to think of it, it's not even funny.

Like most of us guys, I got up for work, left the house and on my way I stopped at a local newsagents for a morning paper and a packet of cigarettes.

Guess what happened next. Don't bother – I'll tell you!

I opened my wallet and . . . nothing – not a brass farthing. I had been mugged! Which brings me to a new statute law that should be introduced.

It's called – wait for it – silent mugging!

This offence, nay *crime*, is committed when you are asleep or, in my case, just drunk!!

Your missus or your kids get up before you and dip your pockets, cleaning you out of everything.

It's about time the police did something about it!

So be warned, my fellow men. The next time you walk into a shop to buy something, or board a bus to go some-where, and discover your wallet is empty, remember what I told you – *silent mugging*!

The Doctor's Bag

. . .

One day, whilst engaged in warrant duties, I had occasion to call at the home of a doctor, with an apprehension warrant for failing to appear at court.

After knocking on the door several times and receiving no reply, I left with a view to returning at a later date.

However, later that day I was patrolling the same area and decided to make another call at the doctor's address.

On arriving at the house, I immediately noticed a car parked in the driveway which hadn't been there earlier.

I called at the door and it was answered by the doctor.

He confirmed his identity to me and I made him aware of the apprehension warrant I had in my possession.

I then informed him he would have to accompany me to the police station.

The doctor appeared somewhat excited by all of this and readily agreed to my request. He asked for a few moments to gather some things together before coming with me.

He then went inside his house and appeared back at the door a few minutes later, carrying a small doctor's bag.

'Excuse me, sir, but, this isn't a house call, so you won't need to bring your doctor's bag!' I informed him.

'Oh, this isn't my medical bag, officer. It's just my overnight bag,' replied the slightly naive doctor, excited by the prospect of an overnight stay at the police station.

'Can you tell me what you have in it, sir?' I enquired.

The doctor opened his bag and replied in all sincerity, 'Just my jim-jams, slippers and my toothbrush!'

I had to control myself from laughing.

I then tactfully informed him, without causing too much embarrassment to the doctor, that his night attire would definitely not be required where he was going.

Public Enemy Number One

· · ·

A second-hand dealer who ran a furniture shop in a busy location received a regular number of fixed penalty parking tickets, for his van being continually parked on the road outside his premises during peak times and for repeated offences of unnecessary obstruction of the foot-path with his furniture.

However, one particular day, his premises had been broken into and several antiques and pieces of valuable property had been stolen.

On my arrival at his premises, I was noting information from the dealer with regards to what had been taken, in order to fill out a crime report, and during my enquiries I asked him if there was anyone in particular with an obvious grudge against him.

Quick as a flash, without holding back, he blurted out, 'Only you bastards! I get on fine with everybody else!!'

Tut-tut!

Laughter – the Best Medicine

...

Whilst seconded to the Crime Intelligence office in the Strathclyde Police HQ, I was working with two regular crime intelligence officers who were both suffering ill health and had been placed on protective duties, but both were exceptional at their respective collators' duties and so they were assigned permanent positions.

One of them, Bob Agnew, apart from contracting legionnaires' disease, had been involved in a motorcycle accident resulting in him being left with a noticeable limp.

The other officer, Jimmy McNulty, had cancer and was attending hospital for regular sessions of chemotherapy.

One day we were having a tea break and the boss at the time was discussing the possibility of recruiting another permanent member of staff to crime intelligence.

As I was currently seconded to the office, I immediately volunteered my services and went into my Yosser Hughes impression and said, 'Gie's the job! I can do it. C'mon, boss, give me the job!'

Quick as a flash, Jimmy McNulty said, 'You can't get a job in here unless you have a gammy leg or cancer, and I would suggest the latter as it doesn't leave you with a limp!!!'

What a sense of humour and outlook on life they both enjoyed. I must say, it was a pleasure working with them!

The Adventures of Harry the Polis

. . .

Bad Time to Ask

· · ·

An unidentified dead male was discovered at the rear of a tenement in the West End of Glasgow.

The circumstances of his death were suspicious and therefore a Special Crime team of officers was set up to make local door-to-door inquiries to try and identify him.

I was partnered off with a fairly young, ambitious and relatively new CID officer.

We knocked on the door of a well-known prostitute in the area.

I discreetly informed my young partner that she was the local hooker.

The door was answered and we identified ourselves to her as police officers making inquiries into the suspicious death of a man found in the area. I then showed her a photograph of the unidentified deceased male.

At this point she invited us into her apartment in order to have a better look at the photograph.

Moments later she handed me back the photograph, saying she didn't know him and definitely hadn't seen him around the area.

As we were leaving, my young partner held back and, aware that prostitutes are excellent for passing on information to the police, he said, 'Listen, hen, any chance of giving me a wee turn?'

To which she misunderstood his request and replied in all sincerity, 'I'd love to, pal, but I can't – my period just came this morning!!'

A Smashing Service

. . .

Whist on police motorcycle duty along with Alex Urquart, my partner, we attended a call to assist an Asian motorist who had locked his car doors with the keys still inside.

We had been issued with 'jiggler' keys, which were thin pieces of key-shaped metal, but, I have to say, I don't know of any police officer who had any success with them, and I know from personal experience that they did more damage to the car locks and ignitions than anything else we had used.

However, Alex said to me to remain on my bike and he would try out the jigglers.

He made the initial effort to open the car door with them, but to no avail. New car – no use!

He was just about to make our excuses and ride off when he noticed a slight gap in the front passenger door window.

As a last resort, he pulled on his leather motorcycle gloves and proceeded to try and slide the window down enough in order to get his hand inside.

Concentrating all his efforts at this attempt, he slid his hand down the car window repeatedly.

I must admit to being quite impressed with the amount of effort Alex was putting into this task to gain entry, as was the Asian car owner and his family, who were all standing around him, pointing, as he worked away like a beaver, sliding his hands repeatedly down the window.

He continued to work at the window using this method and a short time later all of his hard work and effort was rewarded when a small gap appeared at the top of the window.

There was barely enough space to insert his fingers into.

However, Alex squeezed his leather-gloved fingers into the gap and as he did so, he pulled down hard on the window – sssmaasshhh!!! – the window completely shattered under the pressure, scattering broken glass everywhere, inside and out.

Unperturbed by this disaster, Alex nonchalantly put his hand inside the broken window, opened the door and, turning to the stunned, shocked and totally gobsmacked Asian driver and his family, he confidently said, 'There you go, sir. That's the door open for you now!'

He then turned around to face me with a look of horror etched across his face.

At that he walked over to where I was still seated on my motorcycle, looking on in astonishment, and calmly mounted his motorbike.

Starting up the engine, he whispered out of the side of his mouth, 'Quick, let's GTF before he clocks my shoulder number!'

He then rode off along the road without looking back!

Quickly followed by me, I hasten to add!

Screen for Prints

• • •

There was a married policeman who considered himself a bit of a ladies' man and would annoy the other members of the shift with his constant boasting about his latest conquests.

One evening, after being out on the ran-dan, he persuaded a hot female raver to join him for a night of passion in his car.

The following morning, his long-suffering wife had to be up and out of the house early, taking the family car with her.

It was a bitter cold morning and, although she was operating the car heaters, there was a very cold draught blowing like a severe gale from the front of the car.

His wife telephoned him about this and he told her to call in at the local garage to have it checked.

While checking for the heating fault, the mechanic discovered the front windscreen had been pushed out of the rubber seal along the bottom part of the window.

The wife was unable to explain the reason for this but was delighted just to have it repaired.

Having had the windscreen resealed, the wife was leaving the garage and switched on the car heaters.

The windscreen immediately steamed up for a moment with the hot air, revealing a perfectly clear set of footprints on the passenger side.

His night of hot passion in the family car proved his downfall, as his conquest for the night had left her mark, or should I say put her foot in it!

Footnote!

• • •

Which reminds me of the cop who turned up to play football one day wearing a pair of ladies' tights under his trousers.

He was asked by his colleague, 'When did you start wearing women's tights?'

To which he replied, 'Ever since the wife found them in the glove compartment of my car!'

I Don't Think So

• • •

One day, while out patrolling my area, my attention was drawn to an elderly couple and a woman in her thirties.

The elderly man summoned me for assistance and informed me he stayed in the upper flat in a block of four and had locked himself out.

Looking up at their house, I noticed a window open so I said to the man, 'If we can get a ladder, we could climb up and gain entry through the open window.'

He looked up for a moment and then, turning back to me, said, 'Well, I suppose *we* could, but I doubt very much if my wife and daughter would manage it!'

Too Busy To Care

...

Six o'clock in the morning and I had almost finished my nightshift when I received a call to attend a house where an elderly lady had fallen out of her bed and required assistance.

I attended at once and knocked on the door. A moment later, the door was opened by a frail, diminutive woman wearing a bright yellow housecoat and brown bed socks. Her hair was white and tousled with a red patch sticking up at the back. An obvious old DIY dye job on its way out!

From the rear she resembled a wee colourful cartoon chicken!

As she walked up the hallway, beckoning us with her little hand to follow her, I could only smile at this tiny scrawny figure, frightened, lonely and requiring my help.

Once inside her lounge, she pulled herself up on to a fireside chair and stared at the TV programme while swinging her legs back and forth.

I checked with her that she was OK and had not injured herself falling out of bed, while my partner made her a hot cup of tea.

I could tell immediately that she was crying out for some company and the 'falling out of bed' had just been an excuse for us to attend.

'Have you any family, Lily?' I asked her.

'Nope, I haven't anybody at all. I'm an orphan!' she replied, while still staring at the TV and swinging her little chicken legs like a child in nursery school.

'Well,' I asked, 'can you tell me who sent you the lovely cards on your mantelpiece?'

'Don't know!' she said. 'They were put through my door by mistake!'

One said, 'Happy Mother's Day from Grace and Jim'. The other said, 'To Gran from Laura'.

As it turned out, this was her family and I found an address book with telephone numbers of Grace and Laura.

With Laura being the closest address to our location, I called her and explained the situation, asking for someone to attend from the family.

She was concerned for her gran's health, but said that she couldn't attend at this time (six o'clock in the morning) as she had one child of school age and an eight-month-old baby to tend to and was in the house by herself, but that she would attend later.

She then supplied me with her mother's telephone number to call and said that she and her dad would attend.

I contacted Grace, Lily's daughter, and informed her of what had happened to Lily and requested her to attend at her mother's home address.

I had barely finished my sentence when Grace went off at a tangent and began bawling and shouting at me over the phone about how she was sick fed up with her mother and her blatant attention-seeking.

She also claimed her husband, who was due in from his work, was also fed up with 'Old Lily' and her 'Orphan Annie antics'.

As Grace rambled on in my ear, venting her anger at me, I glanced over at Lily, who was sitting like an innocent little child, hair unkempt and sticking up at the back of her head, like Bette Davis in *Whatever Happened to Baby Jane?* She continued to swing her legs back and forth, without a care in the world and totally oblivious to what her 'loving' daughter Grace was saying about her over the phone to a complete stranger.

This ranting and raving by her daughter continued for several minutes: 'I'm a head teacher and have a very busy schedule ahead of me. She's just a frigging nuisance. She's play-acting to get attention. I've tried to put her into a home, but she won't bloody go!'

I tried to interrupt her but she was in full flow!

'I am under a lot of pressure running a busy school and I have the added responsibility for opening it up this morning because the janitor is off sick!'

She also reiterated that her husband Jim was just fed up to the back teeth with her and was seriously considering forcibly putting her into a nursing home to get some peace!

Having listened long enough to the rants of someone who gave me the impression she would be happier if I dealt with her mother and made a decision, I said, 'Right, Grace, I've heard enough! You're obviously too busy to attend your own flesh and blood so I'm just going to arrange to have your mother put down. Goodbye!'

I then replaced the telephone.

Within seconds, it was ringing.

My partner swears he could see steam rising from the handset as I answered it.

It was Grace – surprise! surprise! And she couldn't wait for me to greet her.

'What did you just say to me?' she asked aggressively.

'I beg your pardon, but who is this calling?' I asked facetiously.

'You know fine well who it is!' replied Grace. 'Now, what did you just say to me?'

'Oh, it's you, Grace!' I replied in a positive manner. 'I said you're obviously a very busy woman so I'll just wait with your mother until you arrange to come round!'

'No, you did not say that!' she responded angrily. 'I'm going to—'

I interrupted her in full flow and said, 'Come around, I hope!. Now, as much as I would like to carry on with this conversation, Grace, I do have other calls to attend, so goodbye!'

I then replaced the telephone again.

Turning to Lily, I said my goodbyes and left her in the capable hands of the social services who were now in attendance.

I then buggered off sharpish before old vinegar tits Grace telephoned back or, even worse, made a personal appearance!

However, I often wonder what happened to old Lily, but, more importantly, who opened the school that morning?

Robocop

. . .

A uniformed officer was attending the High Court in Edinburgh to give evidence in a murder trial.

As he was called into the court, he walked forward to take up his position in the witness box, directly opposite the jury.

The judge stopped him in his tracks and said, 'Officer, you appear overly decorated for your appearance in court today. Can you explain to me and the ladies and gentlemen of the jury what you are wearing?'

'Certainly, m'lord!' replied the officer, and he began to explain his police-issue equipment. 'Firstly, I am wearing a body armour vest, to protect and cover my torso. I have a power belt, containing a CS gas canister and holder, a PR24 side-handled extending baton, a Pair of quick-release handcuffs, a set of various keys, including traffic control light keys, my personal mobile telephone, a pouch with a Magnum torch, a pouch with a Wetherman multi-purpose tool, my police notebook, a pouch holder for fixed penalty notices and a police personal radio, wired up my back, with a hands-free mouthpiece and earpiece, m'lord!'

'Is this worn by all uniformed police officers?' asked the judge.

'Yes, m'lord!' replied the officer.

To which the judge said, 'Well, I'm not sure whether I should swear you in or plug you in.'

It's in the Stars

• • •

I was parked one evening in a pedestrian precinct in Glasgow, when I saw a well-known female clairvoyant/fortune-teller coming out of a restaurant where a charity celebrity dinner was being held by astrologers, clairvoyants and psychics.

I watched her as she unsteadily made her way over to a parked vehicle, opened the door and got into the driver's seat.

She started the vehicle up and promptly reversed it into a concrete plant pot in the precinct before driving off.

I quickly followed her and, after a short distance, I signalled for her to pull over and stop, as I suspected she was driving under the influence of alcohol.

I informed her of my suspicion and proceeded to give her a breath test, which proved to be positive!

As procedure dictates, I informed her, 'I arrest you!'

She then looked me straight in the eye with a bewildered, glazed expression on her face and said, in all sincerity, 'What is going to happen now?'

To which I couldn't resist replying, 'You're the clairvoyant – you tell me!!'

Wee Jock

. . .

I answered an advertisement in a local newspaper for a 'Small Scottish terrier, free to good home, house-trained and talks non-stop'!

I couldn't believe the last part so I called the telephone number given and spoke with the owner.

'No, it's not a misprint!' he told me. 'Come and see for yourself!'

This I had to see! I drove my car to the address and the man whom I had spoken with on the phone answered the door.

'Come away in!' he said.

I entered the house and he directed me to a small terrier lying in a basket on the kitchen floor.

'What's his name?' I asked.

'Ask him,' he replied. 'He can speak for himself!'

I felt quite silly at this point. However, I turned to the wee dog, which was now sitting up in his basket looking at me, and said, 'What's your name, then?'

Without any hesitation, the wee dog answered back, 'Jock. Although most people, him included' – nodding his head towards his owner – 'call me Wee Jock! A bit unfair considering I recently sired a big Doberman bitch two doors away!'

I stood there in total amazement. I couldn't believe it – a talking dog! I had to know more and hear his little Scottish voice answering my questions.

'Tell me a bit about yourself, Jock! Like, how old are you? What's your background?'

'Right!' said Jock. 'When I was born, I was the runt in a litter of three. My mother never showed me any true love or attention and blamed me for my father running away with a Border collie who just happened to work in a nearby farm. She claimed it was my fault and I'd put him up to it. Anyway, she had a breakdown after this and went to the dogs — pardon the pun! She began hanging around with mongrel bitches in the area and getting involved in street fights. My brother spotted her having a gang bang with a boxer and his mates on a street corner, the dirty bitch!

'As it was, I ended up being taken into care by a police dog handler, who brought me up with an Alsatian called Rex. It wasn't long before I was allowed to go to work with him and very soon it became clear I had a nose for sniffing out drugs! You name the drug, I've snorted them! So to speak. I would go into an airport baggage hall and within minutes I would have pinpointed all the hold-alls and suit-cases that contained even the least wee bit of drugs. Aspirin! Hash! Coke! Within a very short time I was the dog's bollocks. The chief constable bestowed commenda-tion after commendation on me for the amount of drug crimes I was detecting. I was the Drug Squad's biggest asset! Check my basket, by the way – it's full of police awards. I was getting more publicity headlines than Lassie, in fact. I was even collared and offered a film part in the remake of *Greyfriars Bobby*, playing the lead, no less. Check my basket. Read all the letters. I'm not kidding you!

'Next thing I know, Her Majesty the Queen has contacted the chief constable, asking if I could come down to Buckingham Palace and sort out a few of her young royal corgis, who were misbehaving, peeing and shitting all over one's rugs and carpets. "Not a problem, Your Majesty," said the chief constable, and within twenty-four hours I was whisked off down to England to work in the palace. It was an absolute dawdle working for the royals, and the food was pure nectar. The top chef was that Gordon Setter . . . or is it Ramsay? Y'know who I mean.

'I sorted out the problem in jig time in my own sweet fashion. I introduced a few of the cheeky boys to my Glesca kiss and had a bite at another. I even took the opportunity to have a one-night stand and shagged one they called Fergie – she was a right randy wee bitch. So I've left a wee bit of Scottish bloodline among one's royal corgis. Mind you, I was Corgi registered so I had authorisation! The entire episode was like nothing I'd ever experienced before, waking up every morning between Prince Phil and the Queen. I totally loved it and it didn't go unnoticed with Her (Majesty) indoors either, with the job I had performed teaching they young royal rascals. As a reward, I was recognised in her New Year Honours list. I'm sure you must have read about it! I was in all the papers, Wee Jock CBE (Corgi Behavioural Expert). I was even pictured alongside Sean Connery. However, if you don't believe me, check it out – it's all in my basket and it's stamped with the royal approval!'

I stood there full of excitement, mesmerised by this fascinating wee dog. I was totally in awe of his incredible stories about his life.

'Please, please, Jock, carry on!' I insisted.

I glanced over my left shoulder to catch a glimpse of his owner, shaking his head in disbelief at my eagerness to digest more.

'OK, then!' continued Jock. 'So I'm back home in Glesca, still working alongside the police Drug Squad, when all hell broke loose and I hear all about the Iranian Embassy siege. I couldn't believe what I was hearing on the news. This terrorist mob of murdering bastards were holding innocent people hostage! Sorry for swearing, boss, but I was barking mad. Anyhow, the door bursts open and in comes the chief constable. "Jock!" he shouted. "Prime Minister Thatcher has been on the telephone and she wants you down at the embassy asap, to work in conjunction with the elite SAS."

' "Will they gie me a gun?! Will they gie me a gun?!" I pleaded with him. "Oh, please, gie me a gun and let me shoot the buggers!"

' "Can't do it, Jock!" he said. "The SAS have a special assignment in mind that only you can do! Even I don't know what it is. So good luck, Jock. Go forth and do us proud, son!" He then lifted me up on to his knee, gave me a cuddle, rubbed my chest, patted me on the head and said, "I love you, Jock. Take care!" I got a bit worried about that last remark, 'cause I'd never seen him look at me like that before, never mind uttering the words "I love you". Anyway, off I went to Glesca airport to be flown down south first class, where I was met by Maggie's private secretary and a driver. All very top secret, but that's the way it had to be—'

'Aw, hurry up, for God's sake!' interrupted Jock's owner!

'Hey, you!' said Jock. 'Keep it shut or I'll tell him about the special videos you hide under yer bed for night-time viewing!'

The owner clamped up and stepped back.

'Right now, where was I before I was so rudely interrupted?' asked Jock.

'You had arrived in London and were being driven to the hostage siege at the embassy,' I replied excitedly, engrossed in every bit of the story.

'Oh, aye! Well, I arrived there and was taken to see the PM and her commander-in-chief who was directing the operation. "Jock!" he said, recognising me instantly and delighted to see me. "This is what we want you to do." He then explained they were going to fit a small video camera to my collar. I would then go and locate the cat flap at the rear door of the embassy, whereby I would enter the building and casually walk around the various rooms and floors, videoing the terrorists and their positions in offices for the information of the SAS. As an added extra, whilst carrying out this task and being virtually unnoticed by the terrorist bastards, I was to casually piddle down the left leg of everyone I came across, marking them with my urine.

'Now the boys in the SAS, for their part, would burst in, wearing special nightsight, pish-detecting goggles that would show up my urine like a luminous yellow stain, thereby identifying the bastards to be shot. Easy-peasy! So off I went, through the door, and as I walked up to the first big mother-f****r, nice as you like, Ah lifted my leg and skooshed him. Not one of them paid any notice to me as I wandered about the rooms amongst them like a ghost. In fact, one o' the bastards tried to entice me o'er with a chocolate biscuit, but he was pure mocket and had black teeth! After the initial few squirts down the leg, I was getting right into my stride, showing some neat versatility in the process. I was ambidextrous and showing a variety of special moves, lifting either leg to skoosh the bastards. I kept this up, sometimes double-dunking a particular big diddy that I really disliked, just to make sure he was a target and not mistaken for one of the good guys. I continued in this vein until, inevitably, I had completely emptied my tank! I then came back out, armed with my video pictures of some right pishy-looking terrorists, and gave it to the boys of the SAS to view before preparing to storm the embassy. As soon as they entered, they couldn't miss the terrorists and their bright yellow left legs. It was over in minutes, with the terrorists overpowered and not a hair on a hostage harmed. Thanks to me!

'The Prime Minister was ecstatic! She couldn't believe that Operation Iranian Embassy had gone so smoothly. She cuddled me! Denis breathed whisky on me and that Kate Adie couldn't keep her hands off me – desperate for me to give her one! An exclusive story that is. I ended up back at the palace getting awarded with a bravery medal from the Queen who, along with Philip, was delighted for me.'

Amazed with his stories, I turned to Wee Jock's owner and said, 'Why would anyone want to get rid of this wee dog? His stories about his life are totally amazing!'

At which point, his owner put his hands up to his head in sheer frustration and anguish before screaming, 'It's the *lies*! I just can't take his *bloody lies*!'

Guess Where?

· · ·

The door of the police station opened and in walked a young teenage boy with his hand over his left eye, with blood, visibly from an injury, dripping between his fingers.

I immediately took a sterile pad from the first-aid box and, placing it over his eye injury, instructed him to hold it firmly.

He then told me another youth on the bus on which he was travelling had pulled a knife out and stabbed him.

He described the youth responsible for his injury.

Whilst taking the report, I called an ambulance for the injured youth and a police patrol to stop the bus and arrest the suspect.

Within a very short period of time, I was informed that the youth responsible had been arrested.

Moments later, a young acting sergeant called at the station while the injured youth was still present, holding the bloodstained pad on his injured eye and awaiting the arrival of the ambulance.

Looking at the injured youth sitting there, he asked him, 'So what happened to you, then?'

'I was stabbed,' replied the youth.

To which the young sergeant asked, 'You were stabbed? And where were you stabbed, then?'

I stopped writing at this point and looked at the injured youth, who was looking at me totally confused, and said to the sergeant, 'Why don't you look at his face and take a guess, Sergeant?'

The Perfect Robber
· · ·

A patrol car received an urgent alarm call at 9.30 a.m. to attend a local licensed grocer's shop.

They immediately responded to the call, arriving after a very short time.

As they pulled up outside, the key holder, dressed smartly in a shirt and tie, opened the door of the premises and said, 'My apologies, guys. I set off the alarm by mistake when I was opening up. I did try to cancel you, but your office said you would have to attend!'

The officers confirmed this was standard procedure, just to check that all was well inside.

However, they never went inside owing to the manager, as they thought, having met them at the door with his explanation.

The manager thanked them for their quick response, after which the patrol car left the location, the call to their control room being, 'Staff entering the premises – all in order.'

Later that morning the officers received another call to return to the shop and, on attending, this time they entered the shop to find the staff, minus the bogus manager, tied up in the rear storeroom.

They had been duped by a very cool customer, who was well aware of the police procedure and used it to his advantage to commit a perfect robbery.

However, his luck ran out a few weeks later when the suspect bogus manager was arrested during a disturbance in a lounge bar, after trying to steal a customer's wallet from his jacket pocket while sitting next to him at a table!

The arresting cops took great delight in nabbing him, having instantly recognised him from the previous experience.

Subliminal Thoughts
• • •

Two uniformed cops were walking along the main street when they saw a rather good-looking, well-endowed blonde woman coming towards them, carrying parcels in both hands along with an umbrella.

One of the cops made a remark, out the side of his mouth, to the other about her rather obvious stand-out features.

As she neared them, she dropped her umbrella.

Quick as a flash, one of the cops bent down and picking it up. He said to the woman, 'Excuse me, miss, you've dropped your tits!!'

Realising what he had just blurted out, he immediately tried to correct himself: 'I mean your umbrella! You've dropped your umbrella!'

Too late! He had said it.

Fortunately for him, the woman just smiled, took her umbrella from the extremely red-faced cop and walked off.

As much as he would like to forget the incident, his colleague(s) would not allow him to.

Surely this was the first time that a subliminal thought process was used in the police force, with a 100 per cent success rate!

Police Scotland Exams

• • •

During the police examinations being held at Glasgow University, a mature cop was sitting his sergeants' exam for the umpteenth time, having failed miserably in years gone by.

This time he had made a real concerted effort to do well and had genuinely studied for several months.

During the exam, it was noticeable to those all around that he meant business as he hardly stopped writing.

At the completion, the adjudicator called for all students to stop writing and put their pens down.

Totally ignoring this request, the old cop continued to write on in an attempt to make sure he didn't miss out on anything.

The adjudicator made his way up and down the rows, collecting the completed exam papers, totally ignoring the old cop who was still vigorously writing away.

After collecting all the papers, the adjudicator stacked them in a large pile on his desk as the students, in turn, trundled out of the hall.

The old cop, now finished writing, walked up to the desk and handed his completed exam papers to the adjudicator, who refused to accept them, citing that he had continued writing after being informed to stop!

'Oh, don't be so ridiculous,' he said. 'Do you know who I am?'

To which the adjudicator replied, 'I have no idea who you are!'

The old cop replied, 'Good.' Then placing his hand over

the collected pile of exam papers, he inserted his own amongst them before pushing them over on to the floor and walking out!

CSI Crime Investigation

· · ·

I attended the scene of a housebreaking and while looking at the point of entry, it was obvious to me the house-breakers used a 'true' or 'false' key to get in.

I immediately suspected an inside insurance job by the householder or one of her sons.

I was about to put my theory into practice with the lady of the house when I noticed a piece of paper with writing on it which she had left pinned on the back door of her house for her sons. It read, 'Gone out to the shops, won't be long. Love, Mum. PS: The keys are in the usual place (in the yellow peg bag hanging on the washing line)'!

It's a Knockout

...

Two motorcycle cops were riding along the road when one of them noticed a man on the roof of a bungalow, repairing a TV aerial.

The cop looked away for a second and when he looked back, he saw the aerial dangling from the roof but no sign of the repairman.

'Quick, follow me!' Jack Spratt shouted to his partner.

He then sped off on his bike in the direction of the house.

As they arrive outside the house, they quickly parked their motorcycles and ran around to the back garden, where they found the repairman lying on his back, on the concrete paving, coughing, choking and having extreme difficulty breathing.

Jack grabbed hold of the injured man's shirt lapel and promptly punched him on the jaw, rendering him unconscious.

The other officer, on seeing this unprovoked and extreme action, panicked and blurted out, 'W-W-What the f-f-frigging hell are you d-d-doing, man? Have you gone completely m-m-mad?' Then, focusing on the unconscious man, he said, 'Aarghh! You've killed him! You've bloody killed him!!'

'For goodness' sake, calm down and look at him!' replied Jack. 'Look at him. He's totally relaxed and breathing much more easily now!'

'Oh, aye, he's that bloody relaxed, he's no' breathing at all!' said his partner.

'Aye, he is,' replied Jack. 'See, what you don't know is, he might have broken a rib in his fall and with him struggling to breathe, he could have punctured a lung, so now that he's unconscious and relaxed, he can breathe more easily.'

With the Jack Spratt method of first aid duly administered, they contacted an ambulance to take the man to the local hospital for further treatment.

They told the ambulance crew they would contact the hospital in person to check on his injuries and progress.

They then continued with their previous enquiries.

Later the same day, they returned to the Traffic Department office where they contacted the hospital to ask about the injured repairman.

'Hello there, this is Constable Jack Spratt. I had occasion to contact an ambulance today for a man who injured himself when he fell off the roof of a house in Giffnock. I think his name was Leonard! Can you give me an update on his injuries for my police report?' he asked.

The nurse paused for a moment then replied, 'Right, his name is Liam Leonard and he's been admitted to ward ten – that's the observation ward. He has a fractured jaw and some slight bruising to his body!' she replied.

Jack then paused for a moment, before asking the nurse, 'Are you sure there aren't any other injuries? Like maybe a broken rib or a broken arm?'

'No, nothing else,' replied the nurse. 'Just the fracture to his jaw!' (Courtesy of the polis!!)

Bomb Disposal Man

• • •

Several years ago my partner Donnie Henderson and I received a call regarding a suspicious parcel that had been delivered to a Jewish delicatessen in the Gorbals in Glasgow.

The procedure, we had recently been informed, was to switch off our police personal radios – as a precaution in case they activated a sensor in the suspect parcel – and also to evacuate the immediate vicinity before contacting the army bomb-disposal experts.

'Right, sir,' Donnie said to the shopkeeper. 'Where is it, then?'

The shop owner replied nervously, 'It's on the worktop counter in the back shop!'

'Where did it come from?' Donnie asked him.

'It was delivered to the shop, but I'm positive I heard a ticking noise coming from inside it,' he said, concerned.

'OK,' said Donnie, taking command of the situation. 'Can you please take your staff outside the shop and stand well away, while I perform some basic tests!'

The shopkeeper replied, 'Certainly! Right, everybody outside while the police experts run some tests and check it out.'

Now, I'm thinking to myself, 'What basic tests are these, Donnie?'

'Right, Harry, are they all outside?' he asked.

'Yes!' I replied, desperate to know what his next move was.

'Good,' he said. 'Now stand behind me and watch an expert at work.'

Then, taking out his wooden police truncheon, he stood behind the thin plasterboard wall separating the front shop from the back, looked at where the mystery box was on the counter and, reaching inside with his truncheon, hit the box a right wallop, knocking it clean off the worktop counter.

As it fell on to the floor of the shop, the box burst open, revealing several lengths of extremely dangerous Cumberland sausage.

However, all expertly executed as per the City of Glasgow Police Manual. With one hand covering one's face to protect it from any blast!

Mind you, I suppose if it isn't cooked properly, a Cumberland sausage could be considered very dangerous in the wrong hands!!

By the way, we had a particular 'bomb box' which was retained in the police station and could be brought out at a minute's notice for dealing with such suspicious incidents.

The bomb box was made of wood and half full with wood shavings. Now how advanced was that, then?

However, I can't ever remember it being utilised in any controlled explosions!

Watch Yer Back

...

Once when I was working with 'Soapy' (the Carbolic Alcoholic), we were returning to the Gorbals police station for our dinner break.

I sat down at the table in the kitchen with my sandwich box beside me and began munching away at its contents.

Soapy was pottering about between the rest room and the kitchen.

Moments later, while I was engrossed in reading the newspaper, I heard Soapy behind me saying, 'Now, just hold yer breath and it will be all over in a moment, before you know it!'

My eyebrows raised as I thought to myself, 'Who is he talking to?'

'Are you talking to me? Is he talking to me? He must be talking to me, 'cause there isn't anybody else here!'

A wee bit of my versatility impersonating Robert De Niro there!

Anyway, in all sincerity, he continued, 'I promise you, you'll be straight in and straight back out, so don't worry!'

My suspicions got the better of me and I slowly turned around to see Soapy, standing with a mug of hot water and holding a tea bag in his hand, about to dip it into the mug.

From that day, I never turned my back on Soapy again and I must admit, it raised my awareness and I seriously considered organising a lawful demonstration against cruelty to tea bags! Well, why not?

If they don't get scalded with boiling water, they get hung up by a string and squeezed to death!

Prison Riot

. . .

My brother Freddie related a story that he heard during a golf club function.

The guest speaker was a former deputy prison warden and he was explaining that, while he was an acting governor, staff contacted him regarding a riot in the prison.

He was informed that several inmates had climbed on to the roof and were ripping the slates off and hurling them into the prisoners' exercise yard.

He immediately attended at the prison to assess the situation and was quickly briefed on arrival by his senior officer on duty.

He then went out into the yard, where a few of the trustee prisoners were attempting to clear up the debris.

With the aid of a loudspeaker, he tried to reason with the rebellious inmates on the roof.

All his talking fell on deaf ears as the prisoners ignored his request to come down and discuss matters.

As he stood there, frantically wracking his brain for an amicable solution to this problem, he overheard one of the trustees in the yard say that he knew how to get them down off the roof.

'Why didn't I think of that?' he thought to himself. 'If anybody knows how to get a con off the roof, it's another con himself!'

He nonchalantly sidled over to the trustee and said, 'Tell me something, Coutts – how would you get those prisoners off the roof?'

'Very easily, Guvnor,' replied Coutts. 'I'd shoot the bastards!'

Hair Today, Gone Forever

* * *

There was a wee policeman who I based my cartoon character PC Archie Bauld on who was very vain about going bald and would comb his hair from his armpits across his head.

He would get extremely irate if anybody made a remark about it.

Like: 'You should visit Carpetwise for a new rug!'

Or: 'I'd send that wig back, Larry. It's got a big hole in it!'

I remember we all went swimming one day and he dived in and as he came up to the surface, his hand swept his hair right across his head as he followed through with a crawl swimming stroke. It was priceless to see how well he had perfected his technique and style.

Anyway, I'm sure you get my drift.

One night the entire shift went out to a pub to celebrate with a colleague his twenty-five years in the force.

As usual, we all got very drunk and were having a good time when I spotted Larry in the corner of the pub.

He was so drunk he had fallen asleep and was slumped over a chair, all the hair that usually covered his balding head hanging off the opposite side and almost touching the floor.

As a wind-up, I said to some of the younger cops who had suffered a hard time from Larry in the past and who were eager to get their own back, 'I'll tell you what – if I had a pair of scissors right now, I would cut that bloody mop of hair off and give him a right surprise in the morning when he sobers up and looks in the mirror at his barnet!'

A few minutes later I heard – snip! snip! snip!

I looked over to see Larry being sheared like Larry the Lamb by a drunken young cop.

I swear there was enough hair on the floor to knit an Arran jumper.

As the word spread, the guys came over to see the new-look Larry.

First there was an expression of shock and horror, followed by hysterical laughter!

He looked like the famous barber Sweeney Todd had scalped him!   No, better still, the Irish one – Tom O'Hawk!

Suddenly Larry opened his eyes and surveyed the activity going on around him.

'What's up, Larry?' I asked him.

'I don't know but you're up to something, ya shower o' buggers!' he said with a grin.

As he got up from his seat I asked him, 'Where are you going?'

'I'm going to siphon my python. Is that all right with you?' he replied.

As he entered the toilet there was a rush for the exit door by all the young cops.

As for the haircut, I gathered the remains and put it in his jacket pocket for the morning after! I'm all heart!

Open the Door

. . .

Late one night I received a call that a person wanted on warrant by the police was in a house in Rutherglen.

Accompanied by three other cops, I attended at the address given.

So as not to spook our wanted person, I parked the police van several metres away, out of sight, and we walked to the building to avoid being seen.

The entrance to the tenement had a security entry system with buzzers for each flat.

I buzzed the ground-floor apartment, which had a light on.

'Who is it?' screeched a woman's voice over the intercom.

'It's the police!' I replied quietly. 'Can you let me into the building please?'

'Who did you say you were?' she asked.

'It's the police, ma'am!' I repeated in a soft voice.

'What are you whispering for, then?' she said.

'Because we need to gain entry quietly!' I replied.

'Why?! What's up?' she asked.

'Nothing to alarm you, ma'am. I just require to gain entry to the building,' I repeated.

'Don't you have a key, then?' she asked me.

'No, ma'am, I don't have a key. Now, can you please let me in the building?' I pleaded with her, trying to keep reasonably quiet.

'Well, how do I know you're the polis?' she enquired.

I assured her that I was and she need only look out her window and she would see for herself.

This she did, by pulling her curtain to one side, whereupon she saw my three police colleagues and me standing on the footpath, in full view, waving to her.

She then returned to her intercom and I stood at the door, ready to open it when she buzzed.

'You don't look like polis,' she blurted out. 'Where's yer hats?'

I was becoming exasperated with her but remained very calm.

'They're in the police van!' I replied. 'Now, will you please open the door to the building and allow us access?'

She paused for a moment, then said, 'Whit polis van are ye referring tae, 'cause I don't see one?'

'That's because I parked it further along the road!' I said, trying not to lose my cool. 'Now will you buzz the door and let us in, please?' I repeated for the umpteenth time.

'Why did you park it further along the road?' she asked.

I explained that we didn't want the person we were after seeing us arrive in the van.

Although by this time I think most of the street knew of our presence.

Finally she decided she would let us in, but there was a delay.

'Now what's up?' I asked her.

'It's my buzzer — it's stuck!' she said.

'That doesn't surprise me, missus. You probably don't use it enough!' I replied facetiously.

It was then decided that she would come out to the front of the building and unlock the door, but she would only do it if we stood far enough back from the entrance.

I agreed and we all stood back as she tiptoed to the door, pulled it open and then ran back to her house.

Guess what?

As I approached the door – bang! – it closed shut.

I buzzed her again and told her we did not gain entry, as the door had closed before we could reach it.

'Please, would you mind opening it again?' I asked politely.

As before, we had to stand well back from the entrance.

We were all becoming so frustrated with her that we were going to rush the door as soon as she opened it this time.

It was also suggested we forget about our wanted person and just arrest her instead! Jokingly, of course!!

Finally we gained entry to the building, and guess what? There was no trace of our suspect!

I just wonder how he knew we were coming . . .

The Taxi

...

One day a policewoman colleague overslept for her early shift.

Quick as a flash, she jumped out of bed and whilst pulling on her uniform, she called for a taxi.

Several minutes later she made her way downstairs and was standing just outside the front door, awaiting its arrival, when a Vauxhall Cavalier drove into the street, stopping outside her apartment block.

Closing her front door, she ran over to the car, opened the rear passenger door and got in.

Once inside, she noticed old newspapers, empty Coke cans and chocolate and sweet papers strewn about the back seat and floor.

Annoyed about the untidy state of the car, she said, in a rather indignant voice, to the driver, who by this time had turned around to look at his passenger, 'I think it is about time you had a valet done and washed out the back of this taxi. It's absolutely filthy!'

At which point the rather bemused elderly driver said, 'I'm sorry to disappoint you, hen, but this isn't a taxi. I'm only here to collect my son for work!'

Exit a rather embarrassed policewoman!

It's Good To Talk!

...

A newly promoted superintendent arrived at his subdivisional office to take up his new tenure.

Like all promoted officers on the first day at a new station, he was eager to make a quick impression with the staff.

As he sat down at his desk, he took time to survey all around him.

Suddenly there was a knock at the door.

He quickly picked up the telephone on his desk and put it to his ear, whereby he then called out, 'Enter!'

The door opened and in walked the elderly duty desk sergeant.

The superintendent placed his hand over the mouthpiece and said, 'Be with you in a minute, Sergeant. Just wait there!'

The following is the one-sided conversation that took place.

'Yes, John [the name of a former chief constable]. I'm settling in fine, thank you. What about you? How is retirement? Good, I'm glad to hear it because I know from talking to Willie [the new chief] you're going to be a very hard act to follow!'

The duty desk sergeant stood patiently waiting, looking around the room uneasily and tapping his foot on the floor.

'Anyway, John, I'll have to go now. I've someone desperately waiting to see me – you know what it's like at the top – so I'll speak to you later!'

At that point he replaced the telephone handset and looked up at the sergeant, who is was patiently waiting.

'Right, Sergeant, what can I do for you, then?' he asked.

To which the elderly sergeant replied, 'It was just to let you know, sir, that the engineer from British Telecom is here to reconnect your telephone!!!'

Boozers Get the Bullet

· · ·

If you think Britain's drink-driving laws are harsh, then here are a few other countries with penalties for you to compare.

In Russia they ban drink-drivers for life, while in Norway, Finland and Sweden you'll receive twelve months' hard labour.

The penalty in South Africa is ten years in prison, whereas in Turkey you're driven out of town for thirty miles and made to walk home . . .

But the daddy of them all is in El Salvador, where they shoot you by firing squad!

Recently a driver in Strathclyde only received an eighteen-month prison sentence for causing a road accident in which he killed four people!

By the way, he was sober!!

The Special Bunch

...

At a Christmas dinner dance organised by the Special Branch, at a five-star city centre hotel, things were going with a swing.

The meal was excellent, the entertainment first class and the booze was so bloody expensive there was a financial advisor at every table!

Gone are the days when you could turn up at a function with a 50-quid note in your tail and still have a pocketful of change left in the morning.

One guy in the know said to me in the toilet, 'I've got a monkey with me – will that be OK? What do you think, mate?'

'I don't know what to say, mate. I saw you coming in with yer partner earlier and she looked OK to me!'

'Naw!' he replied, shaking his head. 'A monkey is slang for five hundred quid!'

'Are you sitting at my table?' I asked him.

'I don't think so, mate!' he replied.

'Well, yer monkey should be enough, then!' I said.

After a heavy session on the whisky, from a bottle I cleverly concealed under the table, and I had been up and down like a whore's drawers all night, performing my amazing John Travolta moves on the dance floor, I asked my dance partner if she could smell my Brut. She replied, 'Smell it? I can feel it against my leg!'

With that said, it was time to hit the pillow, while one's legs could still participate in movement by themselves.

I was oozing sex appeal. Unfortunately I was honking like a brewery! Even though I say it myself!

Accompanied by the missus and my two best pals – Whyte and Mackay – I was escorted to my hotel boudoir!

I collapsed on to the bed with my missus, who helped me with my clothing while she nonchalantly dipped my pockets, relieving me of any money I might have left after the hotel bar had relieved me of the lion's share.

Talk of love-making was gone within seconds as the Italian Stallion snored like Porky the Pig!

Suddenly I received a dig in the ribs from the missus and I thought, 'Here we go, foreplay – she must be in the mood!'

I opened my eyes to howls of hysterical laughter from a group of gatecrashers standing around the bottom of our bed.

'Quick, darling, it's the Muppets. Get autographs for the kids!' I said sarcastically. Followed by, 'Get to hell out the room!'

Moments later I ushered them out as they continued laughing and carrying on. I watched as they entered their own rooms further along the corridor.

Next morning I saw the gatecrashers from earlier on, still laughing and joking as they passed me, unnoticed, on the stairs, making their way to the dining room for breakfast.

As soon as I arrived back, I checked their rooms and lo and behold, two of them had been left unlocked. Tut-tut!

All that crime prevention training as well!

I just had to have payback, which I did by relieving both unlocked rooms of their entire mini-bar – whisky, brandy, vodka, gin, cashew nuts and the Toblerone! (No cuddly toy!)

The night they joined my company uninvited proved costly indeed, as I had the last laugh! I just hope they had a monkey with them to pay their hotel bill! SBs (Silly Buggers)!

Look Before You Leap!

...

In the early seventies there was a spate of break-ins at the Linn Crematorium on the Southside of Glasgow, targeted in the Linn Gatehouse, and the items being stolen were BT telephone handsets, which were proving very popular with the thieves.

It was decided that should any urgent alarm calls be received, the attending officers should approach the premises along the extensive driveway, with the lights of the police car out and, if possible, freewheeling with the engine off.

This was because the thieves could see the police approach from a long way off and were able to escape.

One night I was on mobile patrol with Harry Morton and we received a call to attend.

Off we went and, as we reached the main gate, we switched off the lights and engine. We were almost upon them before they saw us in the dark.

When they did, the one standing outside performing his 'edgy', or lookout, ran off into the cemetery while the other was apprehended as he climbed out of the window.

I pursued the one that got away into the darkness of the cemetery. As I did, I quickly caught up with him when he jumped over a large laurel bush, closely followed by me.

'Aaarrrrggghhh!' was the cry as I plummeted over the bush after him.

What a surprise was in store for us both as we plunged sixty feet over an embankment, through branches of fallen trees and into the River Cart below.

And before you ask, no, I didn't emerge with a salmon in my pocket.

I suppose it was our good fortune that neither of us was seriously injured. However, several years later I was to come across the young man whom I took the plunge with, when I attended a road accident in Glasgow city centre.

It appeared that whilst riding his motorcycle in town, he had jumped a red light and was struck by a Corporation bus.

For the second time in his life, he forgot the saying 'Look before you leap', and this time it proved to be very costly as he sustained serious injuries.

Soft Hands

• • •

I received this text recently from my friend Laurie and thought I'd share it with you.

The Fairy Liquid people are filming a new advert for their washing-up liquid, set in the Gorbals.

Here's the script, in typical Glesca dialogue:

'Hey, Maw, how's yer hauns sae saft?'

''Cause I'm only fuckin' thirteen, ya eejit!'

Got It Licked

...

A civilian station assistant telephoned the police station one morning, reporting sick with a head injury caused when he walked into a door. A report was filed in the office 'sickness book' as was the normal practice.

However, later the same day one of the local beat officers happened to meet and speak with his wife, who related an entirely different cause for his head injury.

Her version was as follows. Apparently during the night, while in bed, she had been woken by a noise outside the front door. She quickly roused her husband from a deep sleep and informed him about the noise and told him to go downstairs to investigate.

Up he got from his bed and, wearing nothing but a smile, slipped quietly downstairs to check it out.

Unable to hear anything, he tiptoed over to the door – which had a glass panel with a fancy water design effect on it – and bent over to peer through it.

However, while in this position, bent over, standing there naked, with his nose almost pressed against the glass, he received a sudden fright, causing him to jerk forward and break the glass with his head.

As a result he sustained the cut to his head which required three stitches, and the door required a new pane of glass.

What could have given him such a fright as to cause this, I hear you ask?

Well, apparently while he was standing there in the aforesaid position, his overfriendly Labrador quietly got up from its bed, sidled up behind him and licked his bare arse!!

Road Accident Excuses

· · ·

'I thought my window was down, but I found out, to my extreme hurt, it was up when I put my head through it.'

'The pedestrian had no idea in which direction to run, so I ran over him.'

Haircuts by Tom O'Hawk

· · ·

A beat cop called into his local hairdresser's for a trim.

However, his usual barber was not available and therefore one of the other female staff members took over.

'What would you like?' she asked him politely.

Trying to be funny with the young girl, the cop answered, 'I'll have a Parma ham salad sandwich and a large latte!'

The hairdresser looked at him puzzled and said, 'This is a hairdresser's!'

To which our cop replied, 'Well, give me a haircut, then!'

The girl began cutting his hair.

Snip, snip, snip! Snip, snip, snip!

The hair was falling off quicker than excess pounds at a new WeightWatchers diet class.

Finally, becoming a little concerned, the cop could stand it no more and said, 'Excuse me, hen, did I ask you to give me the worst haircut in the shop?'

Without missing a snip, the hairdresser replied, 'No, but don't worry – I won't charge you any extra for it.'

Animal Crackers

· · ·

An elderly woman contacted the police to report that she had been assaulted and robbed in her house by three monkeys.

As you can imagine, the cops who attended to take the report formed the opinion that she was havering and humoured her.

The following week, the same old lady sustained a broken wrist and bruising to her face.

She informed the hospital staff it was caused by three monkeys who did it while they were engaged in robbing her!

Several weeks later, three men wearing monkey masks were arrested in connection with another incident and admitted to robbing the old woman, who had been telling the truth.

The procurator fiscal arranged for the old woman to be brought to his office in order to go over the statement she had given to the police officers.

He started out by asking her, 'How long have you stayed in the Glasgow area?'

'Three years!' replied the woman.

'And before that, where did you stay?' asked the Fiscal.

'I was in Leverndale [Mental] Hospital,' she answered.

'Do you work at all?' he enquired.

'Yes, I do,' she replied, extremely pleased with herself.

'And what do you work at?' the fiscal asked.

She proudly blurted out, 'I'm an officer in the elite SAS!!'

With that the fiscal looked up at the ceiling.

However, all was not lost – good fortune prevailed and the accused persons pled guilty and saved the procurator fiscal from going 'bananas'!

What Do You Mean?

· · ·

Whilst spending a few days seconded to the traffic speed radar squad, I was asked if I had brought a sandwich with me for my lunch or did I wish to buy something from the local baker's.

I had nothing with me so I opted to go to the baker's with Eddie Weldon and Jock Campbell, two members of the squad.

We all entered the shop together.

'Yes, m'dear, what would you like?' enquired the stout female shop assistant.

I answered, 'A hot pie, please.'

The assistant opened the hotplate cabinet and, picking up a pie, she placed it neatly on to a white paper napkin.

Returning to the counter, she asked, 'Would you like a wee poke with that?'

To which I immediately responded with, 'Not just now, hen, can you no' see I'm still working?!'

Eddie and Jock almost choked at the thought and spent the rest of the day relating the story to everybody we met!

Wear a Hat

...

Alex Black was a senior officer at police HQ and was instrumental in bringing out an order to all police personnel that while driving or travelling in police vehicles, they must wear their hat.

No excuse would be accepted for any officer not wearing a hat and punishment for disobeying his order would be an automatic return to uniformed beat duties.

One day the senior officer referred to called at the station where I was on desk duty.

He was saying how much he liked my private car, which was parked in the yard at the station, and that he was interested in buying one himself.

However, he was apprehensive about the amount of headroom there was!

I sensed he wanted to try my car seating out, but was reluctant to ask, so I invited him to come outside and try it for himself, which he readily agreed to.

Outside in the yard, I opened my car door and he got into the passenger seat.

He sat there for a moment, fidgeting and adjusting his seating position to try and get comfortable, then said, 'There's not a lot of headroom in your car either, Harry, considering its size.'

To which I replied, 'That may be true, sir, but then I wouldn't normally wear my police hat in my private car!'

He then uttered something under his breath as he sheepishly put his hand up and removed his.

Runaway

...

From *The Adventures of Harry the Polis*

Harry the Polis and his young colleague Toby were chasing a suspect who had climbed up on to an eight-foot boundary wall and jumped down the other side in an attempt to make good his escape.

Toby had followed him and climbed up on to the wall and was about to jump down the other side.

Harry sensed danger and shouted at Toby, 'Don't jump, Toby. You're liable to break your neck!'

'No, I won't,' responded a confident Toby. 'I was the college sports champion – I'm a very good jumper.'

'Well,' replied Harry, 'you'll fall and crack your skull, then!'

'I won't! My head is as hard as a brick, and anyway, I'll land on my feet!' was Toby's sharp response.

'Well, you'll break your legs for sure!' said a concerned Harry.

'I've climbed bigger and jumped higher than this wall to worry about what may or may not happen!' replied Toby, disregarding all of Harry's sound advice.

'Right, that's it!' responded Harry rather indignantly. 'Well, just remember, if you break your legs, don't come running to me!!!'

Is Fred There?

...

I attended a call whereby a van had been reversed over a child's bicycle, causing extensive damage to the wheels and frame.

The driver of the van had driven off, hit and run, without giving anyone his name or other particulars.

After making enquiries with the neighbours, one person remembered seeing a van parked with a car registration number similar to that of his own.

Taking note of the registration, I then returned and explained to the woman who had called us that the driver may be unaware of the incident but that we would make all attempts to trace him and make him aware it was a child's bike he had damaged.

Once informed, he would then compensate for the damage to the bike. Not!!

The van registration and driver were easily traced, but when I contacted the driver he flatly denied being there and so refused to accept responsibility for any damage.

He even produced a witness, in the shape of his wife, who just happened to be with him on the opposite side of the city at the time of the accident.

With no witnesses of our own, we had to accept his denial and back off.

However, my colleague David, who was due to retire in ten days' time, said, 'Leave it to me. I know how I'll fix him!'

The following week we began our nightshift tour of duty.

About half past three in the morning, my old colleague, armed with the van driver's phone number, rang him up.

After several rings, the telephone was answered by a sleepy-sounding man.

'Is Fred there?' asked David in a broad Yorkshire accent.

'No, there's nobody called Fred here. You've got the wrong number!' replied the man before hanging up.

Next morning, around 4 a.m., my colleague David called again.

Moments later, the telephone was answered by the man.

'Is Fred there?' David asked again in his Yorkshire accent.

'No, I told you last night – there's no one here called Fred!'

Down went the telephone again.

David continued with this for the entire week, sometimes twice nightly.

The disturbed and tormented man was becoming increasingly upset and angry.

He even told David, in no uncertain terms, where Fred and he should go and take a running jump.

Finally, on the seventh and last night of our shift, David called the van driver again.

This time the phone rang out longer than usual before it was eventually answered.

Just as it was picked up, David said in his Yorkshire accent, 'Hello, there! This is Fred, here. Have you got any messages for me?'

At which point David reckons the telephone was ripped out from the wall socket!

He had administered some summary justice, if only slight!

Taxi Please, It's Raining

. . .

A ned telephoned the police station and said in his broadest Glaswegian slang, 'Listen, big man, I'm over at the hole 'n the wall area and I'm just finishing off a bottle o' Buckie wine. Know where I mean?'

'Yes,' I replied. 'I know where you mean.'

'Right, then, do you know the bus shelter, jist up the road fae it?'

'Yes,' I replied again. 'What about it?'

'Any chance o' sending the paddy wagon over tae pick me up, 'cause it's pishing doon wi' rain and I want tae haun mysel' in!'

'Right,' I said. 'I'm just finishing off a mug o' tea, so do you know where the police station is, wee man?'

'Of course I know where the office is, I've been jailed oaften enough.' He paused, before asking, 'Don't you know who I am?'

'Why?' I asked him. 'Don't *you* know who you are?'

'Who, me? Of course Ah know who Ah am,!' he replied. 'It's me!'

'Well, that's good to know. Now I suggest you get your arse into gear and get yourself over here pronto and you might not get soaked. Although you sound a bit wet behind the ears to me,' I said with a voice of authority. 'Now move yer arse and hurry up about it!'

There was silence for a moment and then he said, 'Whit?! Nae pandas in a polis motor tae come and lift me?'

'That's right, son. Nae taxi drivers. Now move it!' I repeated.

I then replaced the phone, not expecting to hear from him again.

Twenty minutes later the door of the police station opened and in walked this ned. Soaked through to the skin from the downpour, he walked directly up to the front desk and said, 'How's it gaun, big man? It wis me that phoned ye, tae haun mysel' in.'

The Thermal Flask
· · ·

Auld Bob MacDonald turned up for the nightshift one evening sporting a brand new flask along with his sandwich box.

'That's a fancy new flask you have, Bob,' remarked one of the young cops.

'This, son, is not just any old flask – this is a special flask!' said Bob, stirring interest in his young admirer.

'What do you mean, "special", Bob?' he enquired.

'Well,' replied Bob. 'This flask will keep hot things hot and cold things cold, for you to use whenever you want!'

The young cop had a puzzled expression on his face, and said, 'So what have you got in it just now, then?'

Bob replied with a straight face, 'Two ice poles and a cup of coffee!!'

Nurses Can't Be Trusted

. . .

I had occasion to visit my partner Eddie O'Reilly in the Southern General Hospital, where he had been admitted and placed in traction after a serious road accident on his police motorbike.

Whilst on duty, I was allowed to call in and see him outwith normal visiting times.

On this particular day it was not long after the patients in the ward had been served lunch and they were all settling down for a quiet period and the usual afternoon nap.

While I sat alongside his bed talking, O'Reilly interrupted me and said, 'Is the man in the next bed sleeping?'

I leaned forward on my seat to look at him.

'Aye, he's sound asleep,' I replied, unaware of what was next.

'Right!' said O'Reilly. 'Reach over to his locker and grab a handful of his paper tissues!'

'Whit?' I said, surprised, while sitting there decked out in my black leather police motorcycle uniform. 'No way! He might just wake up while I'm doing it and catch me in the act.!'

'He won't wake up – they give him strong medication to make him sleep,' replied O'Reilly reassuringly! 'Now, stop being a drama queen, Harry, and get them for me!'

'Let me get this right – you want me to steal some paper tissues from an unconscious patient on strong medication?' I asked him.

'I've told you, it's no' stealing. You're only borrowing

them for me 'cause I don't want to wake him up and ask him!' O'Reilly replied convincingly.

'Well, OK,' I said reluctantly. 'But if he *does* waken up, you can do the explaining.'

I then leaned over, making certain he was asleep, before grabbing hold of several tissues which I handed over to O'Reilly.

I was somewhat puzzled as to why he wanted them, but oh boy, was I in for a shock!

Taking the tissues in one hand, he reached up with his other hand and grabbed the metal traction framework above his head.

He then pulled himself up from his bed and shoved the hand clutching the paper tissues behind his back.

To my utter disbelief, he wiped his bare backside with them!

He then produced the brown, soiled tissues for me to view and said, in total disgust, 'I knew it! That bloody young nurse isn't wiping my arse properly!!'

He then tried to hand the soiled tissues to me but, by this time, I had buggered off down the stairs, mounted my motorcycle and was halfway along the Govan Road before you could say 'Andrex'.

However, having 'borrowed' the paper tissues, like he said he was doing, I often wondered if he ever put them back.

Yuck!!

Watch Yer Car, Mister?

. . .

On football match days in Glasgow, it was normal for motorists parking near the stadium to be surrounded with a posse of young boys saying, 'Watch yer motor for you, mister? It doesn't cost much.'

Every car owner would be offered their services.

The practice was to agree to their request and give them some loose change from your pocket and they would make sure your car was safe for the duration of the football match.

One day a new Vauxhall Frontera jeep drove up and out got two well-dressed men.

As usual, the posse descended on them, offering their services to the driver.

'Watch yer motor for you, mister?' they asked.

'No, thanks, boys. No need for you – he'll watch it for me!' the driver replied smugly, pointing to a large Alsatian in the rear of the jeep which began barking ferociously at the boys. 'He's a watchdog!'

Both men walked off, hooting with laughter.

Two hours later, and you can picture the look of horror on their faces when they returned to find their jeep sitting up on bricks minus the four alloy wheels.

Under the windscreen wiper, there was a note which read, 'Ye're right, mister, it is a watchdug. It watched us while we blagged yer wheels, ya diddy!'

It's No Joke

· · ·

Cited as a witness at the old Sheriff Court in Glasgow, I was in the witness rooms, which at that time were small, extremely overcrowded and smokey.

I decided to stand outside in the upstairs foyer.

While there, I looked over at a well-dressed, bespectacled gent, leaning over the banister with a worried facial expression.

I instantly recognised him as a famous TV comedian.

'How are you doing?' I politely enquired.

'Not the best I've ever felt, but I'll be happy when this is all over and done with!' he replied.

'Why? What are you here for?' I asked him outright.

'Unfortunately, I had an accident and I killed an old lady,' he replied dejectedly, with a straight face!

I stared at him for a moment, waiting for a reaction, with him being a well-known comedian, but there was no punchline to follow his answer.

So I shook my head and, in a light-hearted voice, said, 'I must admit, I've seen your act!' And nodding my head I added, 'It's bloody murder!'

At which point he looked right through me in disgust, then walked off into another side room.

Here was a comic who obviously couldn't take a joke!!

Mind you, I later discovered he wasn't joking about the accident.

Prisoner Printout

· · ·

It is normal practice when a duty officer takes over from his opposite number on the early morning shift for him or her to activate the prisoner-processing computer, which prints out a list of all the people apprehended in the last twenty-four hours. A copy of this is made available to the divisional commander.

This procedure is performed by typing in a start time and date then a finish time and date for the required period, and then the computer will ask you to confirm by typing in 'Y' for yes or 'N' for no. (Are you following me so far?)

Now most duty officers, having typed the numbers in, automatically hit the 'Y' button – the 'I've typed it in so it must be correct' attitude!

Once the selection is confirmed, the computer begins printing out your request.

Unfortunately for one duty officer, he typed in the wrong year and what he in fact asked the machine to print out was the previous two years' custody records.

Ream after ream of paper spewed from the machine and, as they found out, even if you switch it off, it still retains the previous request in its memory.

So when you switch it back on, it continues to print out where it had left off.

Some fifteen hours later, it eventually stopped printing.

Now who's to blame for the plight of the rainforest, inspector?

Melt in Your Mouth, Not in the Car

. . .

Wee Andy was asked by his wife to drive to the shops and buy some sweets and chocolate for her and his son.

Off he went but, en route to the shop, his car began billowing out smoke and suddenly burst into flames.

As Andy made an emergency stop and attempted to get out of his smoke-filled car, his seatbelt jammed.

As luck would have it, I was passing in a police car and stopped and rushed over to help the panic-stricken Andy, cutting him free of his seatbelt.

We both stood back and watched as, within minutes, the flames engulfed his car.

Moments later, the fire brigade arrived to extinguish it.

I informed Wee Andy that I would require the relevant documents for my police report.

Andy stated that the documents were in the house, so I drove him home.

As we entered the house, his wife, on seeing me, screamed, 'Oh, don't tell me! What's up? What have you done now?'

'Nothing!' said Wee Andy. 'The car burst into flames while I was driving it. It's lying burnt-out along the road. If it wasn't for this officer cutting my seatbelt off to free me, I'd be burnt to a crisp!'

His wife looked on in disbelief, before uttering the words, 'Talking about "crisp" – I hope you remembered to get the wean and me our crisps and chocolates!'

Whit's that Smell?

· · ·

During a drugs raid on a house in Glasgow, the Drug Squad, armed with reliable information, decided the best way to enter the house would be through the front window, as there was a sophisticated locking system fitted to the front door.

Although the house was on the ground floor, the windows were quite high up. However, the plan was for the first cop to take up a position directly beneath the lounge window.

Other officers would create a diversion by hitting the front door, drawing the attention of those in the house. (Damn clever stuff!)

The first cop would then smash the front lounge window before adopting a position where a second cop would run at him and the first cop would give him a punty lift up and through the open window . . .

One slight problem – a big bloody vicious Rottweiler guarding the front lounge!

Undeterred, the second cop decided, 'Let's just go for it!'

Now I must point out that when one is involved in this type of raid, your adrenaline is running high as a kite. You are pumping!

Smash! – open window, first cop took up his position directly underneath.

Second cop started his run and, getting a punty lift up, he jumped straight through the broken window.

The Rottweiler got such a fright that its bomb doors opened and it shat itself.

At which point the cop, pumping with adrenaline, grabbed hold of it by the arse and neck, picked it up and threw it right out through the broken window.

As he did, piss and shit were flowing freely from the dog's rear end, like muddy water from a burst pipe!

Splat!! It dumped all over the first cop, still in position under the window.

Splat!! It splashed all over the footpath immediately in front of him and – splat!! – on hitting the ground, the big dog was off up the road quicker than a safe bet at the Shawfield dog track!

However, while the dog was on its way out of the window, a third officer had already started his charge towards it.

Splat!! He trod on the dog shit dumped on the footpath!

Splat!! He stood on the hands of the first cop, who was giving him the punty lift up!

Splat!! He then stood on his shoulder, which already had doggy poo all over it!

The first cop was oblivious to what was being spread all over him, or where the obnoxious, foul stench was emanating from . . .

That is until after his adrenaline levels dropped and the drug raid was over and all the house's occupants had been arrested, when his colleagues politely pointed it out to him!

He was then made to sit in the back of the police van along with the accused! Phew!!

Who Are You – Pinnochio?

. . .

One Monday morning, while working dock duty at the High Court in Glasgow, I was having a cup of tea when I looked up and saw a pretty young policewoman coming towards me.

'Hi, Uncle Harry. I bet you're surprised to see me,' she said.

It was the daughter of one of my closest friends.

'What are you doing here?' I asked.

'I've been assigned here for the entire week!' she replied.

She sat down and I introduced her to the other cops present — some of them knew of her dad.

After exchanging some updated gossip with her, I went to see the duty officer and arranged for her to work with me for the rest of the week, as she was a nice, quiet, reserved girl.

I then phoned her dad at his CID office and told him I was working with her and I would make sure she would be all right.

Later that day, we had just come down from the court for lunch and, as usual, had to pass a cell full of accused prisoners due up in the court that day.

As we were passing, one of them shouted out, 'Hey, sweetheart, gonnae sit on my face?'

Quick as a flash, she responded, 'Why? Is your nose bigger than your penis?'

The other prisoners burst out laughing at this impromptu reply and, as we walked on, he was being pelted with verbal abuse from his cellmates!

Blue Grass in Nashville

• • •

Alfie was a recovering alcoholic and a very good friend of mine. He was also an excellent tradesman/joiner/carpenter, having been self-taught.

In the early days, when I first met him, he worked for a ceiling company, installing suspended ceilings.

When I say he worked for a ceiling company, I should add that there was an owner and there was Alfie, who was the main and only workforce employed.

Alfie would work all the hours going and, owing to his excellent workmanship, he was inundated with jobs.

This was great for the owner of the ceiling company, but after a while Alfie would go on a bender, sometimes lasting several weeks, or at least until all his hard-earned money was spent.

If you were as hard-working, good-natured and easily led as Alfie, there were always plenty of un-employed, lazy, scrounging bevvy merchants hanging around like a bad smell, ready to help him spend his cash – or should I say drink it – and as often as not steal it from him.

Anyway, after the umpteenth heavy bender, Alfie found himself in the hospital, suffering from a serious drink-related illness.

This wasn't his usual recovery session – this time it was more serious.

Alfie was informed very bluntly by the consultant that the damage he had inflicted on his frail body was near-fatal and he was extremely lucky to still be alive.

He was also told that, owing to years of continual alcohol abuse, he was at the Last Chance Saloon.

One more drink could prove fatal.

At last – this was the first time Alfie had acknowledged he had a serious drink problem and it was now big decision time: 'Do I want to live or do I want to die?'

A quick check of his underwear after being given this terrifying news convinced Alfie he didn't want to exit from this life just yet.

The only exit he craved at this crucial time in his life was one from his over-excessive and habitual lifestyle.

This decision no doubt upset many of his dependent scroungers in the area.

Having defied the odds and survived, Alfie set about taking on the hardest fight ever, trying to live a normal healthy life like you or me without an alcoholic drink.

The obvious problems were still there, but Alfie found support in his family, his true friends and the excellent assistance given by Alcoholics Anonymous!

A few years on and Alfie was showing signs of great recovery. He was working for himself and performing more hours than the work's cat, with no days off.

This, in hindsight, was Alfie's therapy, keeping his mind and body occupied and regularly attending his AA meetings to keep himself topped up with the help he required to combat his addiction.

Anyway, all work no play can make Jack – or in this case Alfie – a dull boy.

So Alfie decided to venture abroad for the first time in

his life and have a holiday in the USA. This would satisfy his burning ambition to visit Graceland, the luxury home and museum of his all-time, lifelong hero, the late, great legend Elvis Presley – the King!

However, not being the type of person to do anything simple, Alfie decided to hire a car and drive his way across America, visiting all the states, cities and towns on his must-see list.

All very well, but Alfie had just passed his driving test and here he was taking on an enormous venture, particularly having to drive on the opposite side of the road, the opposite side of the car and with an automatic transmission into the bargain.

'Easy-peasy!' said Alfie. 'I'll pick it up as I go along. I'll manage! After all, I've already been to hell and back!'

Alfie went confidently on his way to soak up the experience of a trip he could only have dreamed of through the bottom of a glass at one time in his life.

As well as going to the home of his idol, Elvis, and recording the visit on his camcorder, Alfie decided to leave his mark. After photographing the statues and gates with his treasured Glasgow Rangers scarf draped over them, he etched his name, 'Alfie McGrory', with 'Rangers FC' underneath, on the wall of remembrance for visitors to sign.

As he carried on with his travels, he made his way to the home of country and bluegrass music.

On his arrival in Nashville, there was a massive music festival on (well, *that's* a surprise!) and Alfie decided to go and soak up the atmosphere.

After a short while, Alfie went to the coffee bar area for a much-needed cup of refreshing tea and a cigarette.

As he was served his tea, Alfie was directed over to the bar area where the milk and sugar were.

He went to pour some milk into his tea but the jug was empty. Just at that point a well-dressed, made-up woman with long black hair and nifty country and western style clothes walked past.

Quick as a flash, Alfie put his hand out to stop her and said, 'Here, doll, any chance of some mulk for my tea?'

She looked at him with a puzzled expression on her face and replied, 'Nothing to do with me, sweetheart. See one of them gals behind the counter!' She then walked off.

Fortunately one of the said gals supplied Alfie with some milk but, unfortunately, as Alfie went to light his cigarette, she informed him there was no smoking inside the venue and he would have to go outside to have his cigarette.

Alfie walked outside and stood beside a well-groomed man in fancy cowboy clothing with a necktie to match.

Alfie looked at him and said, 'How's it goin', pal?'

The man replied in an elegant American drawl, 'It's going reasonably well, thank you.' He then paused for a moment before continuing, 'My name is George,' and offered his hand for Alfie to shake. 'With an accent like that, I take it you come from the old country. Am I right?'

'Naw, ye're wrang, big yin! I'm Alfie and I come fae Scotland! I'm only here oan holiday!' he replied.

'Right,' replied George, 'that's what I meant. So are you enjoying your time here, then?'

'Aye, but the service could be a wee bit better. I mean, I

asked the waitress woman for some mulk for my tea and she more or less ignored me!' said Alfie.

Just at that point the fancy-dressed woman Alfie was referring to walked outside.

On seeing her, George greeted her. 'Hi there, Loretta!' he called out.

'Oh, hi there, George!' she replied before continuing on her way.

'That's her!' said Alfie. 'The woman fae the coffee bar that I asked for mulk.'

'Oh, you must be mistaken, my good friend. That lady there is Miss Loretta Lynn. She is one of our finest country and western female artistes!'

'I thought that wis her, but I was just making sure!' Alfie replied, trying to bluff his way out of it. 'Aye, ye're right enough. I recognise her noo, George, but I was just checking, just checking!! I used to be a bit of an artist mysel', you know.'

'Did you really?' enquired George, genuinely interested.

'Aye, a piss artist!' joked Alfie.

The punchline went right over the top of George's head as he looked at Alfie, pondering his next question.

'Are you a fan of bluegrass music, Alfie?' asked George.

'Oh, aye, man. I'm a big blues fan. Huge, in fact! Ah never have it off. It's without doubt my favourite music!' Alfie replied, somewhat unconvincingly. 'Particularly bein' a Rangers fan!'

'And who would you say is your favourite bluegrass artist, then?' asked George.

Quick as a flash, Alfie blurted out, 'Sydney Devine!'

George hesitated for a moment then said, 'Sydney Devine? I don't think I've heard of him before. At least I can't recall the name. Are you sure he is a bluegrass artist?'

'Most definitely,' retorted Alfie. 'I'm surprised he's no' here because he plays in all the big concert halls and community centres around Scotland.'

Just at that, a young man came outside and said, 'I've to tell you five minutes, Mr Hamilton!'

'OK, thank you, Tim!' George said, acknowledging the call. He then turned to Alfie and said, 'As they say in the business, Alfie, the show must go on!'

He then shook Alfie's hand again before disappearing back inside the venue.

As Alfie stood there mulling things over, he looked at the young man who had just joined him and was lighting up a cigarette.

'Who wis the big man, by the way?' he asked Tim.

'Who, the man you were just talking with? Why, he is a huge name in country and western music. That was the one and only George Hamilton the Fourth!!'

Alfie nonchalantly shrugged his shoulders and said, 'Aye, ye're right there, pal. That *is* a huge name. Mind you, if he's the fourth, where's the other three, then?!'

Pillow Talk

• • •

As I was socialising at home with some friends, my four-year-old son Scott walked into the room and shouted over to me, 'Dad, Dad, I need a piss-piss!'

My friends began laughing at this outburst.

I got up from my seat and took Scott out of the room and into the toilet.

While there, I said to him that it was very rude to say what he had just said and in future, if he required the toilet, he should say, 'Dad, I need to whisper!' This was much more polite. I then returned him to bed.

In the early hours of the morning, Scott awakened me from a deep sleep.

'Dad! Dad!' he said, pulling at my arm.

'What's up, son? What's up?' I enquired from my drowsy broken sleep.

'I need to whisper, Dad! I need to whisper!' he replied.

Totally forgetting my earlier lecture, I said, 'OK, son, whisper in my ear, then!'

And he did!

Talk about 'brainwashing'!

Gaun, Ya Dancer!

• • •

It was the norm, when a newly appointed recruit joined the shift, to welcome them by taking the pure mickey!

In other words, you would wind them up.

One day a young policewoman recruit walked into the muster room to meet with her new shift.

As it was, the detail that day partnered her with me so I took her out on patrol.

I was asking her about her family, what she worked at before joining the police and what her hobbies and interests were.

She told me her name was Diane, she was single, and her first passion was dancing, having studied it from a very early age and having won everything there was to be won. She was now teaching ballet and tap to primary school children.

'Ballet dancing?' I said with interest. 'Now, that's quite a coincidence because see Stuart Munro who is on our shift? His mother is quite a famous ballet dancer and she also teaches her own school, but at a very high level!'

'Does she? Oh, I would be interested to know more about her,' she said, quite excited at the prospect.

'Yeah!' I said. 'Well, why don't I introduce you to him? I'm positive he'll be chuffed about the dance connection. In fact, I think his mother received a CBE recently in the Queen's New Year Honours list for her Bolshoi involvement!'

'Bolshoi! Gee, that's amazing!' she enthused. 'I'm sure I must have heard of her.'

Later that day we called back at the station for our refreshment break.

While we relaxed in the rest room, the door opened and in walked Stuart.

Eager to make an impression, Diane went up to Stuart, put out her hand to introduce herself and said, 'Hi there. You must be Stuart. I'm Diane. I believe your mother is a bit of a Bolshoi ballet dancer?'

Stuart looked at her straight-faced, and then a look of utter disgust crept over his face as he said, 'I don't know what your game is, but my poor mother is disabled with polio and has been confined to a wheelchair since she was nine years old!'

Diane's smile turned to a look of total horror as she stood motionless, staring at Stuart.

It was all too much for her to comprehend and moments later she was off and running from the room in tears towards the ladies' restroom.

Stuart then turned to me as his look of disgust suddenly changed and he burst out laughing uncontrollably and said, 'That was pure brilliant! Did we set her up or what?! You've got to admit, that was the best reaction we've had from any probationer yet. What do you think yourself?'

'Definitely, she gets ten out of ten for that reaction!' I said, before falling about laughing hysterically.

How cruel we are at times!

Curry Fever

...

One day I phoned the Police Courts branch of the High Court in Glasgow. The phone was answered by Paul, the duty officer, whom I would regularly wind up.

In an Asian accent, I said I was calling about the interview 'for de chef job' and what time should I come?

Paul advised me that I had contacted the wrong extension and was about to transfer me . . . when I interrupted him, 'Oh, please, please, sir, don't cut me off. I am very good chef and many people are loving my cooking!'

'I'm sure they do, sir, but this is the High Court police cells you've called,' Paul replied.

'But please, sir, this is the number they give me. I especially cook some curries for you to taste. Can you not smell them over de phone? They are delicious,' I said rather convincingly.

'I think I can, sir, but it's the restaurant you really want. They—'

I interrupted Paul again. 'You know what? I have many references from all my neighbours on the stair landing, because I am making them all de curry and I feed them children to, you know, you know!' I said, deliberately talking in broken English.

'Look, sir,' responded Paul, 'I'm sure you're better than the chefs we already have in the court restaurant, but I have absolutely nothing to do with employing them and—'

I quickly interrupted him again. 'You're not believing me, I know it. You think I not good chef and I am feeding all my neighbours! They know I am very good chef!' I said, sounding very upset.

'Not at all, sir,' said Paul apologetically. 'If I could give you the job then I would, but it's not—'

'Did you just say you would give me job, sir?' I asked.

'Yes, I did, sir, without hesitation I would give you it, but—'

'Well, that is bloody marvellous, sir! I have the job, then. Fatima, Fatima, come quickly! I have job – the man on de telephone has given me job! Oh, sir, I am thanking you, I am thanking you so much and Fatima, the mother of my children, is thanking you also at the same time!'

Now suddenly Paul is getting panicky and trying to interrupt me.

'No, no, wait, sir. You misunderstand me – I can't—'

'Oh, sir, my wife and children are so very much excited. Aren't you, Fatima? Fatima is nodding her head, sir, she is so excited. Oh, I can't wait to start. When do I come?'

By this time Paul was totally exasperated and pissed off trying to explain to me. He decided to say anything that would get me the hell off the phone!

'That's good – I'm so happy for you and your "Fat-Ma". Now, I want you to start tomorrow morning, OK? Tomorrow morning!'

He then put the telephone down on me.

However, I then called him straight back and in my own voice I said, 'Hi, Paul. Is that the Job Centre for Asian curry chefs? I hear you're doing interviews for the High Court restaurant.'

Paul responded thus: 'Harry Morris, you bastard!!'

A Mars a Day

...

Having received a report of a naked man standing at his lounge window exposing himself to young girls, I attended, accompanied by my partner, Stevie Mac.

On our arrival at the location we took brief statements from the four female witnesses then went to call at the naked man's door.

After several minutes of intense banging on his door, an elderly fat man, wearing only a massive pair of grey underpants, opened the door to us.

I informed him why we were there and asked to come in.

Once inside, I noticed there was a small wooden stool, strategically placed at the front lounge window for him to stand on, allowing him the height he required for his exposed privates to be seen from the footpath outside.

The room was also full of X-rated videos and pornographic magazines.

Several times, while we were in the house, the smug man made mention of the fact that he was diagnosed with diabetes (the significance being that a diabetic, owing to this condition, cannot have an erection).

However, satisfied with all the evidence, we arrested and conveyed him to the police station.

Steve was very keen to write the police report, and afterwards he handed it to me to check before submitting it to our newly appointed female shift sergeant.

I read over Steve's report, which was fine, but, knowing the female sergeant would scrutinise every paragraph, I decided to add an extra section: 'Remarks to the procurator fiscal. The accused stated that he suffered from diabetes and therefore, as a result, he was virtually unable to obtain an erect penis, unless he consumed two Mars bars, a tube of Smarties and a bottle of Irn Bru prior to and during sexual foreplay!'

I then returned the report to Steve for him to submit, which he did, completely unaware of my extra comments.

Moments later all that could be heard was, '*Steven McNicol! Come to my room now!!*'

Bargain Bombers For Sale

· · ·

I met a police officer from the RUC in Northern Ireland at the police convalescent home in Auchterarder.

We became good friends and, as a result, kept in touch with each other. I went over to Ireland to meet up with him and he showed me around the area where he lived.

One day I decided to go out into town for a spot of shopping.

I found it rather ironic to come across a shop, advertising in bold letters, in the window: 'SALE! SALE! SALE! Large selection of bomber jackets in stock'.

I had a bigger laugh later when I was telling Billy about it and he failed to see the funny side!

Holidays at Helensburgh

...

I was recently reminiscing about family holidays with my younger sister and I related a story to her that she was too young to remember.

As far back as the late fifties and early sixties, I can remember our family holiday consisted of one day away to Helensburgh.

Our wee mammy would make up all the bread sandwiches and Abernethy biscuits, along with flasks of tea and bottles of ginger, and there would be plenty of them to feed my three brothers, two sisters and me.

Then we would all be bundled into the back of my dad's Ford van and off we'd go on our one-day holiday.

Going to Helensburgh required us to cross the River Clyde on the Govan ferry.

I have never seen a ferry crossing yet, because my parents were that badly off for money, my brothers and I had to hide under an old sheet or blanket in the rear of the van to avoid having to pay the ferryman the extra pennies for us. It made our holidays. Especially going home with our collection of whelks and mussels!

Can You Not Take a Joke?

• • •

The former chief constable, Sir Patrick Hamill, walked out of police headquarters one day and headed for his car.

On seeing him, the police commissionaire doorman, Leslie Rose, walked over and opened the car door for him.

As it was, I had parked my police motorcycle outside the front door, immediately in front of his car.

As the chief approached his car, with door held open, he took a detour and walked over to my motorcycle and pretended to mount it.

On seeing this I said to him, 'With all due respect to you, sir, I don't think you could get your leg over that machine!'

Quick as a flash, Chief Constable Hamill said, 'Is that right? Do you know where Shettleston police station is, Mr Morris?

'I do, sir,' I replied.

'Good,' he said. 'Then you can just report there at seven o'clock tomorrow morning!'

He then turned around and entered his car and was driven off.

To this day I hope he was only joking and confirming to all of us present that there was humour at the top of the police ranks.

'Cause needless to say, I didn't bother to report at Shettleston!

The Pink Slip
. . .

A regular occurrence on a Wednesday morning was being bombarded at the police station by members of the public claiming to have lost the cash from their benefit giro cheque on their way from the post office to the shops!

They never, ever lost their giro cheque – it was always their money, immediately after they had cashed it.

Should this unfortunate incident occur, the practice was to call at the local police station and make a loss report, then obtain a 'pink slip' receipt confirming that you had reported the loss. Then you would present your pink slip at the local DHSS office and receive a crisis loan for the amount you allegedly lost.

Whether anyone ever repaid the crisis loan is another story!

The cops and station assistants were becoming more frustrated and infuriated, in particular with the same old faces presenting the same set of circumstances, every other week, as to how they lost their giro money.

One loser came up with a novel excuse which just has to be shared.

Having called at the station, under the influence of alcohol, he reported he had lost his giro cash.

When I asked him where he had lost it, he supplied me with the following account, in a slurred and drunken Glaswegian voice.

'Right, big man, I'm gonnae tell ye the whole truth, right!' (Well, that's a good start!) 'This is absolutely genuine, big man. Ye're never gonnae believe it! Just wait tae Ah tell ye this! See, I've cashed my giro, right? . . . And I had a right dose o' fuckin' toothache. Oops! Sorry for swearing, big man – just a wee slip-up! Anyway, Ah had a right dose o' the effen toothache!'

He then put his hand into his mouth. Pulling it open and pointing with the other hand, he said, 'That bastert right there! Well, it's no' there noo, 'cause it's oot, but I'm telling ye whit happened, big man, as God is my' — hic! — 'judge! Right, so Ah said to mysel, "Dentist, my man—"'

He paused for a moment to think, then repeated, 'Dentist?'

He screwed his eyes up and scratched his head while talking to himself. Then he snapped his fingers!

'Ah mean, "Dennis, my man." Forgot ma fuckin' name there for a minute! Oh, sorry, man, jist slipped oot! Sorry! Anyway, Ah said tae mysel', "Dennis, you need to go and see the dennist!" So I goes to the Dental Hospital, right? And yer man the dennist says tae me, "Dennis, ye're needin' a few out, son, so, I'm gonnae gie ye a wee dose o' gas, OK?" Noo, I cannae argue wi' the guy, 'cause he's a big b-ba-ba—'

I interrupted him before he said it again: 'Dennis!'

He continued, '. . . ba-balack guy, so Ah said tae him, "You're the boss, big man. Fill yer boots, but jist don't shrink my heid!" Right? Well, when I've woke up, my gub was full o' blood and I was feeling like I'd just puffed some heavy Moroccan wacky backy, 'cause ma heid's pure dizzy, right? And this is whit Ah think happened! Noo, listen up. Ah think I've taken my giro money oot and when I went tae put it back into my poacket Ah've missed and it's dropped oot oan tae the grun' below! Whit dae ye think yersel', big yin? Does that no' sound like a pure genuine story?'

He then threw his hands out from his sides and said, doing a Tommy Cooper impersonation: 'The whole truth, big man, just like' — hic! — 'that!'

I stood staring at him for a moment, in total amazement, trying to digest this remarkable tale of woe, which was, in fact, one of the best I've ever heard.

All the while he stood there in front of me, demonstrating with his hands – how he could have missed his pocket? – and then, pulling at his mouth, opening it wide to expose this black crater where he once had teeth. I then said, 'So, you're saying you lost your giro money when you were at the dentist having some teeth removed. Is that right?'

He snapped his fingers then, offering me his hand to shake, said, 'Ye're absolutely spot on, big man. That's exactly whit I've been tellin' ye.' Hic! 'Now ye're talking!'

'Well,' I said, 'might I suggest you rush home to your house and check under your pillow and see if the Tooth Fairy has been? Because you're not getting a pink slip from me!'

Who Let Them Go?

. . .

One day at police headquarters, I had arranged a visit for a local Boys' Brigade outfit.

While I escorted them around the office, taking them into fingerprinting, the taped interview room and the cells, some of the boys wandered off into a room by themselves.

On the wall of this room were photographs of men under the heading: 'Top Ten List'.

'Who are they?' asked one small boy.

I said, 'Those are photographs of the ten most wanted men in Scotland!'

The same small boy, pointing at the wall, enquired again, 'They're the ten most wanted men in Scotland?'

'That's correct,' I replied forthrightly.

'Well,' said the young boy, pausing for a moment, 'don't you think it would have been a good idea to lock them up when you were taking their photographs?'

Don't you just love kids?

Stuck on You

· · ·

Big Alex was a colleague of mine who, along with the rest of the shift, was having a hard time from the inspector.

This senior officer, who had an obvious dislike for everybody, including Alex, was making his life a misery.

On the other hand, Alex was a big gentle giant who got on well with all his colleagues.

Like everything in life, you get to a breaking point when enough is enough, and Alex reached his during one particular nightshift when he asked for some time off to deal with a personal matter.

The shift sergeant, having checked the roster, agreed to his request but the inspector declined it, stating that his absence would deplete the shift and he was already short of shift members.

Therefore Alex's request was refused.

This was the last straw for big Alex and some of the shift, particularly when they heard the inspector had arranged for himself to perform a dayshift while the rest of his shift were working nights.

They decided to seek revenge on the inconsiderate inspector for his bullish tactics and blatant unpopularity amongst the men.

So, during one of the shift nights, big Alex discreetly obtained the private keys to the inspector's office and disappeared inside for a short while.

Oh, to have been a fly on the wall the following day when the inspector entered his office and found everything on his desk was stuck fast to it — his telephone, his family portrait, his fancy paperweight, pens, pencils, desk diary, desk lamp, ashtray, paper tray, etc., etc.

Needless to say nobody owned up to it, but big Alex was thereafter nicknamed 'Superglue' by his fellow officers!

A name that stuck with him for the rest of his police service!

Sign Here

...

When I was part of a Scottish folk band, we toured to Moscow.

Part of our itinerary involved making a personal appearance at a press conference in Pushkin Square.

After a televised interview, which was well attended by numerous young Russians, seeking autographs, our 'fans' surrounded us.

One young man came over to me and handed me a small piece of paper and a felt-tip pen.

He then turned around and patted his shoulder.

Convinced he wanted me to sign my name, I began to write on the back of his fancy shirt, where he was patting.

I had only written Harry and was just beginning to write Morris when he turned around and screamed at me, 'No, no, no! Not here!' (All over his good shirt.)

Then, pointing to the piece of paper he had handed to me at the start, he said, 'Here!' meaning I was to use his back to support the paper while signing!

Too late, young man, too late!

Big Davy Provan

...

While performing another of my many football team escorts, while on motorcycle duties, Ronnie – nicknamed 'the Itch' because he got under everybody's skin – accompanied me.

We were escorting the Irish team Dundalk to Ibrox Park in Glasgow.

Once at the ground, we both went upstairs for a cup of coffee and a nosy about to see who we could recognise.

As we entered the players' lounge, I instantly recognised some of the former players of yesteryear and began talking with some of them about the forthcoming game with Dundalk.

The Itch, not being football-minded, stood sipping his coffee and listening intently to our conversation.

At one point he whispered in my ear, 'Who is that you're talking to, Harry?'

I whispered back, 'It's Davy Provan!'

After a few minutes the Itch interrupted Davy while he was speaking and said, 'You look much taller and so much different in real life!'

'Thank you!' said Davy. 'I'll take that as a compliment!'

Then the Itch turned to me and added, 'Mind you, I think he looked better with his curly hair. What d'you think?'

At which point I replied, 'Wrong Davy Provan! Wrong Team! And wrong era!'

The Handyman

· · ·

From *The Adventures of Harry the Polis*

A new janitor took up his post in the police station.

'Are you the new janitor?' enquired Harry.

'Handyman, son, no' janitor!' he replied indignantly.

'Oh, good,' said Harry. 'Can you fix the plug on the kettle?'

'Sorry, son,' he said. 'I don't touch anything with a plug – that's taboo!'

'OK,' replied Harry. 'How about changing the ceiling light bulb?'

'I can't, son, I've got vertigo and get dizzy up a ladder!' he replied.

'Well, how about seeing if you can fix the lock on the stray-dog kennel?' asked Harry.

'Again, son,' said the jannie, 'fixing locks, that's not my thing – that's a job for a locksmith!'

'I thought you said you were a handyman!' said Harry.

'I am, son!' he responded. 'I just live around the corner!'

Lucky Tatties

...

I was recently reminiscing with my brother Allan about sweets we used to buy, like MB Bars, Whoppers and Milk Dainties, and we brought up the subject of Lucky Tatties.

Now, for those not old enough to know what a Lucky Tattie was, let me explain that it was a brick-hard, flat brown thing, covered with brown powder, which you had to bite through and try and chew. Eventually you would find, concealed inside it, a key ring, a glass marble (jorry) or some other ridiculous little toy.

The 'Lucky' part was that you didn't break your teeth while trying to bite it or swallow the article inside it and choke to death!

Another piece of food we used to eat was my granny's home-made dumpling.

It was brilliant but, for some reason, when mixing it up the ingredients to bake, she would add some silver three-penny coins in the mixture. What was that all about?

In one piece alone, I got three. Mind you, I swallowed two of them. Everybody would say, 'Away, ya lucky wee bugger!'

Lucky?! My granny just tried to choke me with coins and I'm 'lucky'? Don't think so! Imagine one of them stuck in yer gullet.

I had to check my stools for the next few days until I passed them and even then, with the aid of some liquid paraffin, they came out that fast and hard they nearly cracked the toilet pan.

And to crown it all, when I told my mother what I had just passed, she took them off me.

Lucky?! Lucky my arse!

Daytrip to Girvan

...

Ring-ring! Ring-ring! Ring-ring!

'Hello? . . . Oh, you're joking! . . . Ask them to wait for us – we're on our way . . . Quick, everybody, get up! We're late again!'

A voice called out, 'We're late again?'

'That's what I just said! Now, c'mon, you lot, get ready as quickly as you can – the bus is going to wait for us!'

Everybody in the household was frantically rushing about trying to get dressed.

'Where's my other sock?'

'Is your face washed? I don't think so – get back in there and this time use soap and water!'

A voice called out from a nearby bedroom, 'Can somebody please get me a nappy for the wean? We're going to be late again!'

'What do you mean, *going* to be? We *are* late again!'

I checked to see how they were all getting on.

'Somebody get a mirror and check and see if your granny is still breathing. If she is, make sure she's up and getting dressed.'

At that point, Granny entered the room.

'Ah'm up and Ah'm leady!' she slurred.

I looked at her. 'Oh, no! Has anybody seen the mug with your granny's false teeth in it?'

'I think Kimmy had it, Dad!' replied Scott.

'Thanks, son.' I called, 'Kimmy Morris!'

'Wart, Dard?' replied Kimmy.

As I turned around, Kimmy was standing in front of me, trying hard to smile.

'Kimmy!' I shouted. 'Get those teeth out of your mouth and give them back to your granny now!'

'Chan a' no weer thim?' she muttered with difficulty.

'No, you can't! So take them out now and stick them in your granny's gub! You don't know where they've been!'

Yes, readers, it was the local community police families and underprivileged children's annual daytrip to Girvan, and, for the second year running, the Morris family had overslept.

The other area community cops and their families were all waiting outside the police station, where the big orange bus was parked, waiting to whisk them away for a day of races, fun, ice cream, prizes and the odd nervous breakdown by the parents and park rangers.

The driver of the bus must have weighed about twenty-three stone and he loved weans – he couldn't eat a whole one though, but loved them just the same.

He had a 1950s Bill Haley kiss curl (no hair – just a kiss curl!) and an expired Atkins diet certificate displayed on his dashboard.

At 9.55 a.m., some twenty-five minutes late, the Morris family arrived.

Five minutes later and we were off on our trip.

The noise emanating from the excited weans was absolute bedlam but, above it all, you could hear a voice as clear as Quasimodo's bell-ringing.

It was Maggie Mulligan, the CID equivalent of Helen Mirren!

She was also the female clippie for the day.

'All those aboard, get yer money oot tae Ah collect it and make sure ye huv the right change!' she cried out in her own inimitable *Prime Suspect* style.

Turning around, she pointed at one of the wee boys and said, 'Ho, you, Ringo! Sit oan yer wee jazz drum! I don't want tae see anybody staunin' oan the seats. Ye keep that for the hoose!'

The chief organiser, big Joe Logan, lent vocal support. 'Aye, ye heard oor Maggie. Noo dae whit ye're tellt or else!'

He was barely finished speaking when one of the kids called out, 'Hey, look, a big field! We're oot in the countryside already. Let's look for some coos.'

'Away, ya wee diddy. That's a golf course and no' Blythswood Square!' another responded.

'Right, then,' a kid called out. 'Let's see who is first to spot a supermarket trolley in a parking area or in ra burn!'

Another shouted out excitedly, 'Hey, Maw, there's a good three-piece suite dumped at the side o' the road. Did ye see it, Maw? It looked a belter — better than oors.'

You just cannae beat those underprivileged kids and their Glesca patter. Well, certainly not without a big stick!

They're just full o' it.

Big Joe Logan had to have a word with the driver about his choice of music, pointing out that if anybody was the 'Leader of the Gang' it was him and not Gary Glitter!

A short time later, doon through Ayr and we were nearly there! (Ho! That rhymed – I'm a poet and I didn't know it!)

At last we'd arrived at the Victoria Park and, as with all good daytrips, it was raining cats and dogs!

'Watch you don't step on that poodle – I mean puddle!'

'Daddy, can I qui?' asked my son Scott. Scott was getting French lessons at school but I knew what he meant!

'Certainly, son, follow me!' I replied.

Aaarrggghhh!!! Disaster!!

The toilets were locked and there was a queue of weans, all bursting for a pee!

It was like a scene from *Saturday Night Fever* – they were all wriggling about, holding their boabies tightly, trying to prevent leaks.

Some of the auld yins from the bus joined in, thinking they were doing the Slosh or the Alley Cat!

Desperate times call for desperate measures.

'Quick, everybody, close up and form a big circle around this tree, facing inwards. Right, all together, one, two, three – zips down and go for it! Son, try not to wet the person opposite you. Face inwards. Ho, what are you two playing at?' I asked a couple.

'Seeing who can pee the highest up the tree, mister!' they replied.

'Well, just don't let the minister see you, 'cause he'll hit the roof!' I said.

'Shit, he must huv played it afore, the cheat,' they answered back.

One wee boy was facing outwards.

'Ho, wee man, everybody can see your boaby. Face inwards!' I told him.

'But I need a wee Greyfriar's Bobby!' he said desperately.

A moment later Ian Cartwright arrived waving a key and announced, 'Right, then, who needs the toilet?'

'Ye're a bit late with the key, Ian!'

Maggie Mulligan's voice could be heard above everyone else, 'Right, you pair of monkeys, get doon aff that tree! And you buggers, stop fighting or I'll gub the both o' ye!'

She turned to big Joe Logan and said, 'I think we'll feed them noo afore they really get oot o' hand.'

'Aye, ye're right, Maggie. Go for it!' responded big Joe.

They gathered all the kids together.

Joe said, 'Right, everybody, form an orderly queue and collect your packed lunch. And remember, it's only one each! Maggie, will you give the drinks out?'

There was a mad rush as all the weans charge forward to get there first.

During the rush, old Granny was knocked over.

Maureen Conroy had seen this. 'Hey! Take yer time, you lot! You could have hurt that auld yin there and one of us would have been lumbered with having to take her to the hospital! Nae offence, Granny!'

After pigging out, all the weans were at last stuffed. They even refused extras, they'd eaten so much.

Now it was time to clean up the mess they'd made in the park.

They were all running around, collecting the rubbish and discarded food.

'Excuse me, Mr Morris. I picked up this doggy pooh thinking it was a chocolate muffin. What shall I do with it?' said a wee girl.

'Eugh! Don't eat it, that's for sure. Put it down and go and wash your hands thoroughly! And tell your mum.'

I then announced to all the kids, 'Don't pick up any discarded chocolate muffins that have steam coming off them!'

Moments later Ian Allan called everybody to come together.

'OK, children, can I have your attention? It's time for the sports competition. We have some wonderful prizes to give to all the winners!'

That said, they began with the races but they were short of eggs for the egg and spoon race because some of the kids were wearing them as a yolk – I mean joke – having decided on an egg fight.

Then disaster struck as, one by one, the children were dropping out of the competition and spewing and vomiting all over the place.

Some of their faces were the same colour as the Victoria Park grass. All you could hear was 'Ruth!', 'Ralf!' and 'Hughie!' I'm not sure who they all were but we need more tissues over here please!

For over half an hour it was total pandemonium, with all the community cops having to tend to the sick children who were honking.

However, three children in particular were extremely sick, all from the same children's home in Castlemilk.

Why?

The reason became crystal clear when the younger brother of one of them helped himself to a swig of her 7-Up, and it was discovered that they had laced it with vodka. And what we had thought was Ribena turned out to be Buckfast!

David Holland was summoned over to the pitch and putt hut to see the park assistant, who was detaining two of the children.

Apparently the little angels had stolen some golf balls from the rear of the hut and were caught throwing them at the swans in the boating pond, shouting 'Duck!' as they threw them.

Didn't they know the difference?

David apologised for their actions and marched them away to deal with them!

In the meantime, I was playing it low key, trying to merge with the scenery in the park, when all of a sudden Scott and Samantha came running up, looking for me. 'Dad! Dad!'

'Over here kids,' I called out. 'What's up now?'

Out of breath, they blurted out, 'Dad, it's Kimmy! She's jumped over the barrier into the wishing pond with all her clothes on and is collecting all the money in it!'

I rushed over with them to the wishing pond and, sure enough, Kimmy was like Disney's Little Mermaid with a Dyson, hoovering up every coin in the pond.

I was more worried that she would fall over and drown, unable to get up due to the weight of the coins she'd collected.

'Kimmy!' I shouted with authority. 'Put that money back now and come out of there at once!'

'Not on yer life, big man. I found it first!' she replied. 'Remember what you told us? Finders – keepers, losers – weepers!'

'That was a wee rhyme,' I said as I stepped over the fence and lifted her up and over the barrier. 'Give me the money you collected and I'll put it back!'

'That'll be right! The minister doesn't give it back to me on a Sunday when he collects it!'

She then ran off, dripping with water and weighed down by her newly acquired coin collection.

Maureen Conroy approached and announced, 'Right, everybody, Maggie wants you to board the bus, 'cause it's time to go to the hotel for our evening meal!'

That seemed quick. Doesn't time fly when you're enjoying yourself?

However, by this time appetites were back and everyone converged on the bus. It resembled a queue at an EasyJet check-in.

Everybody was wanting a seat at the front.

Bill Hayley, the bus driver, had a job controlling the rush. 'Ho, you, midget! Oot o' there, that's mine. I'm driving the bus!'

David called out, 'Is everybody here? Put yer hand up if ye're not!'

Everyone accounted for, we drove off.

Big Joe had to ask Bill Hayley to turn down his Johnathan King CD of 'Everyone's gone to the Moon.' I bet he was sorry he wasn't there now!

We made the short journey to the hotel, where the staff were expecting us and had arranged all the seating.

The meals couldn't come quick enough as the entire party of community cops and children devoured everything available, including the odd place mat and the pattern off the plates.

Big Joe Logan gave a speech on behalf of the section, promising that there would be another community police trip next year, and then he enthused about the excellent behaviour of all the children in our care.

'Wis he there?' we all asked!

He must have been suffering from selective amnesia.

Or he was a secret drinker! C'mon, Joe, spill the beans!

I then spoke up and assured everyone who had witnessed Kimmy's swimming prowess in the wishing pond that all the monies collected would be donated to Children in Need.

Mind you, Kimmy was muttering something else about a new bike under her breath.

Well, this was, as they say, the Last Supper for us as we all reluctantly made our way on to the big orange bus waiting to take us back home to normality.

Big Joe had to ask Bill Hayley to turn down his tape of Michael Jackson singing 'Billie Jean' so the kids could rest.

As we arrived back at our starting point, many of the little cherubs, mine included, were sleeping, God bless them!

Unfortunately they had to be woken in order to take them on the short journey home to their beds.

As for me? Well, I buggered off sharpish, along with some of the other community cops and a few mothers, to the local police social club for a well-deserved glass of Whyte and Mackay to relieve the tension and stress caused by the community police daytrip to Girvan!

Help Ma Boab

...

Whilst working in the Community Involvement section, I had collected some pencil and rulers with the slogan 'Don't talk to strangers', along with Dennis the Menace badges and stickers about drugs and various other bits and pieces.

I would visit the Boys' Brigade, Scouts and Girls' Brigade, warning them of the dangers and handing out freebies to the kids.

One particular time, I had a roll of luminous yellow posters to hand out to an OAP church group meeting later the same week. These posters said on them in bold letters, 'Help! Call the police!'

I was sitting relaxing with my family, watching a video, when we heard a loud banging coming from outside our patio doors.

I pulled back the curtains and got the fright of my life to see four big uniformed cops staring in and torch lights being shone all around my house.

What was up? What was wrong?

The answer was simple – my seven-year-old daughter Kimmy had found the large yellow posters, intended for the OAPs, and had stuck one up in her bedroom window, alerting all passers-by to: 'Help! Call the police!'

Wacky Races

...

One nightshift, they police support unit were out patrolling in their minibus.

The passengers in the back were discussing which member of the team was the fastest runner.

Was it 'Speedy', wee Bobby Tait, or 'Flash', big Willie Wilson?

The team were divided 50–50.

It was time to settle it once and for all!

They drove to a nearby industrial estate and stopped in a car park behind a large retail store.

Out they got from the minibus and the challengers stripped off their body armour and utility belts to prepare for the race.

The excitement was unbearable as bets were placed.

Both runners lined up (that's a lie – I'm just trying to hype it up).

The sergeant steadied them: three, two one, go!

Off they went at full toot, one end of the car park to the other.

Their legs were like pistons! The result – a dead heat!

'Right,' they said, 'Let's go for it again!'

They lined up for a second time: three, two, one, go!

This time, as they sped across the car park, they were almost at the finishing line when a call was received over their personal radios: 'Would the support unit personnel holding their own version of *Chariots of Fire* please vacate the area, as G Division officers are taking observations in the area due to a recent spate of housebreakings!!!'

Sumjerk Ramdmakhar

...

As I was able to impersonate various accents, the cops in the office would ask me to make calls for them to wind up someone in another office or department.

The cops working out of one office were fed up with the way a particular civilian assistant dealt with the public and wanted me to set him up.

I decided I would call him and report a hit and run road accident with an Indian accent.

The telephone was answered by my victim.

'Strathclyde Police Pollokshaws. Can I help you?'

'Hello, sir. I am wanting to report a car has just collided with my car and de driver is trying to drive off!' I said.

'Where are you, sir?' he asked.

'I'm here in de telephone box calling you!' I replied.

'Yes, I know that, sir, but where?' he repeated.

'Where de telephone box has always been – in de same street where my car has been hit!' I replied sarcastically.

'Right, well, let me put it to you this way – where has your car been hit, then?' he asked.

'On de side of it – big bash, dreadful damage to my car. My wife, she's very upset by this big bugger!' I answered back.

Becoming slightly frustrated by my evasive answers, he said, 'Sir, as much as I appreciate what you are saying, I need to know the name of the street where the accident has taken place.'

'Well, vhy didn't you just ask me that first?' I rudely replied.

'I did, sir, but you obviously misunderstood me,' he said.

'I don't remember you asking me that. Maybe you are talking too fast for me to understand you!' I responded.

By this time I could hear him breathing heavily and could picture his face, with steam coming out of his ears.

'OK, sir! Can . . . you . . . tell . . . me . . . your . . . name . . . please?' he asked sarcastically.

'My . . . name . . . is . . . Sumjerk . . . Ramdmakhar! Do . . . you . . . understand . . . me?' I replied.

'There's no need for that attitude, sir!' he said.

'Vell, you started it!' I answered back.

'OK, let's not argue about it . . . Mr Sum-jerk Ramd-ma-khar! Is that how you pronounce your name?'

At this point the penny dropped and I could hear him repeating the name to himself, under his breath, 'Sum-jerk Ramd-ma-khar! Some jerk rammed my car! Right, you bastard, who is this? I'm on to you!'

'I'm begging your pardon, sir, but why do you call me bastard?' I asked.

'You know exactly why, you bastard. Anyway, I know who you are!' he said, annoyed by the wind-up but more so that he had been duped.

However, if you buy de book, you will know who Sumjerk was!!

And it wasn't me!

Christmas Party

. . .

This is another little story which I just had to include.

I took two of my kids, Samantha and Scott, to the divisional police Christmas party at a local hotel.

As I walked in, there were two young women dressed up like Santa's little elves.

They introduced themselves to their young captivated audience, giving their names as Nik and Nak.

They performed a short routine which they finished off by having the children join them in singing 'Jingle Bells', to herald the arrival of Santa Claus.

However, Santa Claus, along with his good friend 'Rudy', as he liked to be known, was the red-nosed drunk on the shift and had taken a detour through the lounge/cocktail bar en route to the party. Surprise, surprise, he turned up with Rudy smelling of alcohol and both totally pished!

With Santa now possessing a natural red nose just like Rudolph's, the committee decided that Santa and Rudy required a breath test and the children's Christmas party required another Father Christmas.

They ran around frantically trying to arrange a fat replacement to take over the role of Santa.

Meanwhile, they had to ask Nik and Nak to prolong their act and keep the kids amused.

Nik and Nak decided to kill some time by getting some of the kids to tell a story or a joke.

'Who can tell a funny story they've heard or a funny joke?' they asked.

Several of the kids immediately raised their hands.

'Right, that little boy there!' said Nik, pointing to my son Scott.

As I was totally unaware of this, one of the other dads said to me, 'Ho, Harry, is that your son going to tell a joke?'

I turned around in time to hear Scott ask the assembled children and parents, 'How do you make a snooker table laugh?'

'We don't know,' said Nik and Nak. 'How do you make a snooker table laugh?'

To which Scott replied very loudly for everyone to hear, 'You put your hand in its pockets and tickle its balls!!'

I promptly informed the parents nearby, 'That was his granny who told him that one!' before I performed some magic and disappeared! Under the nearest table!

Road Accident Excuses

• • •

'I had been driving for forty years when I fell asleep at the wheel and had an accident.'

Coming and Going

. . .

Whilst on motorcycle duty, assisting with traffic control at another football match in Glasgow, I was riding along the road when I saw a car in front of me that was full of football supporters.

I noticed that the reversing lights were on, while the car was driving forwards.

I decided to stop the car and make the driver aware of the offence!

As I was about to do so, the car was driven across the road on to the opposite carriageway and stopped at the kerbside.

The driver then got out and disappeared into a nearby shop.

I pulled up alongside the passenger door and signalled the male occupant to roll down his window.

I then informed the passenger to tell the driver, on his return, that his reversing lights were stuck on!

The passenger, with a puzzled look, said, in typical Glaswegian, 'That will make absolutely no difference to him, boss.

'He doesn't know whether he is coming or going at the best of times!!'

The Visa Application

...

One afternoon, as I had just taken up duty in the station, the front door opened and in walked a very well-dressed, respectable-looking woman with two equally well-dressed teenage girls.

I asked how I could be of assistance and the polite woman began to explain that her family were intending to visit South Africa on holiday but that she had been informed that she would require to call at a police station to obtain a form of some kind, in relation to their application for a visa.

Having not the slightest idea what she was on about, I informed her I would have to seek the assistance of a colleague.

I explained that he would know what to do, having just returned from South Africa and having experienced problems during his own visit, on arrival and, more importantly, on departure!

Delighted to know there was someone who understood the problem, the woman said, 'That would be wonderful, officer!'

I then called out, 'Constable Stevie McNicol, can you report to the front office immediately?!'

You had to be there to see the look on her face when at the front office arrived a tall black policeman!

'Yes, 'Arry, what can I do for you?' he asked in a deep voice.

You just can't beat a good black comedy sketch, I say!

A Tight Situation

. . .

A motorcycle colleague and I were patrolling Springburn when we were signalled to stop by a concerned female home help.

She had called at the home of one of her elderly lady clients and was unable to gain entry.

However, the elderly lady's Labrador could be heard whining and yelping inside, but none of the neighbours had seen or heard her.

I accompanied the home help to the tenement building, but I was unable to see inside the windows as the curtains were drawn.

I made enquiries as to who might have seen her last and how long the dog had been yelping, but nobody could shed any light on the old lady's recent whereabouts.

I had to accept the fact that she may have suffered a sudden illness or injury and collapsed unconscious.

The first obstacle I encountered was to try and clear the letter box all the newspapers stuffed into it.

I was then met with the wet, heavy panting of her excited dog, which was obviously desperate to get out.

All the while I was positive I could hear a weird moaning sound coming from inside, but it certainly wasn't coming from the dog.

I decided to refrain from wasting any more precious time. There was no other option but to force entry, as I feared she might be lying severely injured.

After several attempts, using bodily force and kicking the door, it finally succumbed to my size nine Doc

Martens. (These Docs were responsible for demolishing many a door.)

The poor desperate dog forced its way past everybody out onto the landing to get to the back door and out to the garden for a long overdue pee.

My colleague, Ian Thomson, and the home help both feared the worst for the elderly woman and prompted me to enter the house first and check for her.

As I made my way along the small hallway, checking each room in turn, I suddenly arrived at the kitchen.

Looking inside, I couldn't stop myself from smiling.

'Are you OK, hen?' I asked the frail figure lying on the kitchen floor staring back at me.

'I think so, but I've lost the feeling in my legs. I think I might be paralysed. I can't move them!' she replied.

At this point I summoned the home help.

After a short chat, a hot cup of tea and a massage to get the blood flowing in the lady's legs again, she was able to tell me that after her supper the night before she was sitting on a small stool in the kitchen, pulling on her warm thermal tights, when she somehow managed to squeeze both feet into the same leg of her tights.

She then forced them on so tightly that she couldn't move.

She had stood up, lost her balance and fallen over on to the kitchen floor.

Thinking that she was paralysed, she lay motionless on the kitchen floor all night.

No doubt the first job for the home help that morning was to go out and buy another pair of thermal stockings!!

D'you Fancy a . . .?
. . .

A trial at the High Court in Glasgow was hearing new evidence from a victim regarding her rape ordeal at the hands of the accused.

She was asked by the advocate depute to tell the jury the exact suggestive remarks and obscenities used by the accused towards her prior to the vicious sexual attack.

The young victim stated that she was embarrassed to repeat the sexually suggestive remarks in public.

In order to assist her in giving this important evidence, the judge suggested she write it down on a piece of paper which could then be passed around the members of the jury for them to read for themselves.

The victim agreed to this and wrote down the suggestive sexual remarks made to her by the accused. She then handed over the note for the judge to read.

Having read the remarks for himself, the judge then handed the paper to the court usher to pass among the jurors.

Each juror in turn read the note, folded it, then passed it to the next.

Eventually it reached a young attractive blonde juror who, having read over its contents, folded the note and, as she made to pass it on, noticed the male juror next to her had his eyes closed, having fallen asleep.

Without attracting too much attention to him sleeping, or causing any fuss, she casually nudged his arm.

The male juror quickly roused and looked at the young attractive woman who had nudged him.

She then raised her eyebrows and passed him the folded note.

The man, oblivious to what had gone before, opened the note and read it, after which he looked at her, smiled and winked.

He then folded the note and promptly put it into his jacket pocket.

On seeing the juror do this, the judge said to him, 'I'll have that piece of paper, please.'

To which the juror replied, rather indignantly, 'I beg your pardon, m'lord, but with all due respect, it's private!'

You're Nicked

. . .

Having received numerous weekly complaints from a local MP about the number of car drivers exceeding the speed limit along the road past his house, my partner and I were sent to the location in order to use the Muni-Quip speed gun.

The speed gun was hand-held. You pointed it in the direction of oncoming traffic and it would register on a small screen the speed of the vehicle.

After several minutes of setting up and checking our equipment, we were set to begin operating.

Moments later our first car arrived at excessive speed. I pointed the speed gun at it and — Bingo! — it registered 44mph. My partner signalled the oncoming driver to pull over and stop.

The driver was made aware of why he had been stopped and shown his registered speed on the screen, after which he said, 'But you can't charge me! I'm the local MP for the area who wrote in and complained about the number of drivers speeding!'

'Well, sir!' I replied, 'you'll be able tell your constituents and write in and inform my supervisor that you saw at first hand the police officers in attendance, performing their duty and catching the offenders!'

Diplomatic Corps

• • •

As a police motorcyclist, I worked with an officer who had a reputation as being quite difficult to work with and was slightly dour-faced.

We were both working at a football cup final in Glasgow, assisting in traffic control, when a football supporter slightly the worse for drink approached.

The following conversation took place.

'Hey, big man, whit kind o' bike is that?' enquired the supporter.

'A big one,' replied the cop.

'I know that, big man, but whit's it called?' he tried again.

'A polis motorbike!' replied the cop.

'Och, I know that, Jimmy, but whit I want to know is, whit make o' bike it is?' persisted the frustrated supporter.

'How did you know my name was Jimmy?' enquired the cop.

'I just guessed!' replied the supporter, pleased with himself.

To which the cop replied, 'Well, you can just bloody guess what make of bike it is as well, can't you?'

He then started his bike up and rode off!

As a footnote to this story, the cop involved was transferred to the Community Involvement branch not long after this particular incident.

Who said we're not hand picked for certain jobs, then?

Popeye for Short

. . .

A man charged with drink-driving attained the services of a well-known and distinguished Scottish solicitor.

During his initial interview, the solicitor noticed his client had an artificial eye, which would play a relevant part in his trial.

The lawyer, while reading the case notes, looked at his client and asked him if he would be prepared to take his artificial eye out, if requested by the lawyer, in a crowded public court?

The accused replied he would be prepared to do anything that might help his case!

The day of the trial arrived and the police witness was being led through his evidence by the procurator fiscal.

After he had given his evidence to the court, it was the turn of the defence to cross-examine him!

The defence lawyer questioned the officer on several points, before asking him to describe the condition of the accused when stopped by the police.

'Well,' said the policeman. 'His speech was slurred, his eyes were glazed and his clothing was dishevelled!'

'You say his eyes were glazed?' repeated the defence lawyer.

'That's correct, sir,' replied the officer.

'Would you take a look at my client, please, and tell me if you think his eyes appear glazed today in court?' asked the lawyer.

The policeman looked across the courtroom and tried to focus on the eyes of the accused in the dock.

'I can't really tell from here, sir,' replied the officer.

'Well, by all means, officer, step down from the witness box, walk over and have a closer look,' said the lawyer confidently.

As the officer was about to step down from the witness podium, the lawyer stopped him and said, 'Better still, stay where you are, officer!' and then, turning around to his client in the dock, he held out his hand and said, 'Can you let me see one of your eyes, please?'

The accused produced a clean white handkerchief from his jacket pocket then, plucking his artificial eye from its socket, placed it on the handkerchief before handing it over to his lawyer.

The lawyer turned to the police officer and, holding the handkerchief up to his face, said, 'Tell me, officer, does this eye appear glazed to you?'

The policeman focused on the artificial eye in front of him then, after pausing a moment, said, 'I can't say for certain, sir, but if you would like to hand me over his other one, I'll compare them!'

Pale Face

• • •

In the motorcycle section we had a daily ritual – you would enter the sergeant's room and sign yourself on duty as you collected the keys for your motorcycle.

The sergeant at the time was John Brown, who was a nice guy but a bit bullish in his supervising.

I found out very quickly that John was a worrier and so I would enter his office each day and as I was signing on duty, I would give him the slightest of glances then look back at him and, in a concerned voice, ask, 'Are you all right, John?'

This would immediately alarm him but he would respond positively, 'Yeah, I'm fine. Why do you ask?'

As I continued to sign in, I would reply, 'No particular reason! I just thought you were looking a bit pale. But you're feeling OK, then?'

John would now stand up and walk over to the mirror on his wall to see his reflection.

'Yeah, I'm feeling all right, I guess!'

'Fine, then,' I would say as I left the office.

Once outside, I would stop the next motorcyclist going in to sign on and tell him what I had said and to carry it on.

By now John would be having another check at himself in the mirror, as the next cop would enter the office.

'Morning, gaffer!'

As he would look at John in a startled way, he'd say, 'Gee whizz, John, are you feeling all right? You're a bit pale looking.'

This would continue with a few more cops and, in a very short time, we'd have convinced John he was not well and he would be off home to his bed.

As a result we'd have peace for a few days until he'd return, feeling much better no doubt!

Shall We Dance?

• • •

While walking along my beat one day, a woman walked up to me and said, 'Can you dance?'

I said, 'Dance?'

She said, 'Aye.'

I said, 'Who?'

She said, 'You.'

I said, 'Me?'

She said, 'Aye.'

I said, 'Naw!' before walking off, totally confused.

Elvis Lives

• • •

After his umpteenth road accident involving a police car, a certain police officer was transferred from the mobile patrol department to assisting the station counter staff.

His fellow officers had cruelly dubbed him 'Elvis' because he had more hits than the Beatles.

One day I was over at the office with a prisoner I had apprehended and Elvis was working at the charge bar, processing the prisoners in the computer.

I asked him, 'How are you enjoying working at a computer?'

Without pausing or lifting his head, Elvis replied sarcastically, 'Well, put it this way, I must be doing OK – I haven't crashed it *yet*!'

It's in the Bag!

. . .

I received a call one day to attend a large superstore in Renfrew Road in Paisley, regarding a male detained for shoplifting.

On my arrival at the store, I spoke with the store detectives who'd witnessed the theft and obtained the necessary statements.

I then asked the store security guard, 'What did the accused steal?'

'A lawnmower grass box,' replied the witness.

I then met with the accused shoplifter and I had to satisfy my curiosity, so I asked him, 'Why are you stealing a grass box?'

He replied, 'Off the record, boss, I'm a professional shoplifter and, between you and me, I blagged the lawnmower yesterday for a punter, but I didnae notice there was a grass box wi' it, so I came back today tae get it and some bastard grassed me to the security in the car park!'

'How much do you earn shoplifting?' I asked with interest.

'I make a good living, stealing to order,' he replied proudly.

Puzzled by his response about the grass box, I had to ask him how he had managed to walk out of a store with a large power lawnmower without anyone in security noticing.

He winked at me and replied, 'If I tell you that, boss, you'll want my job!'

I then winked back, placed my handcuffs on his wrists and said, 'Don't think so!'

Car 54, Where Are You?

· · ·

I worked with a giant of a man called Kenny Morrison from Paisley.

Kenny had moved from the Paisley Burgh police to join the Glasgow traffic department, which was now amalgamated under the new Strathclyde Traffic Police.

Kenny and I formed a good partnership and worked well together.

During one nightshift, we were short of supervisors and Kenny thought he would be asked to perform the duty of acting sergeant.

However, to his utter disgust and disappointment, the traffic headquarters sent over an older cop from Paisley, known to Kenny and cruelly nicknamed 'Granny' Watson, to supervise.

This did not go down well with big Kenny and I was later to learn there was a history of bad feeling between them.

As a result, Kenny was like a bear with a sore head.

Part of the supervisor's duties was to go out in a traffic car during the shift and if he did not come across the traffic cars patrolling their areas, he would call them up on the radio for their position. He would then ask them for a suitable location in order to rendezvous with them and sign and date their police notebooks, as per procedure.

Granny called us up for our location and Kenny promptly replied, 'Carmunnock village!'

The reply came back from Granny, 'OK, I'll rendezvous with you there!'

Now this would not normally be a problem, but we were in Govan at the time.

So I asked Kenny, 'Is it me or do you have a slight problem with your geography?' Carmunnock village being at least eight miles from our present location!

'Nope!' he said. 'But he'll know the entire Southside of Glasgow before this night is over!'

A short time later, while we were still in the Govan area, Granny called on the radio that he was now in Carmunnock – where were we?

Kenny then replied, 'Please note we are now at Shawlands Cross.'

'Roger!' said Granny. 'I'll see you there!'

A short time later, we were still in Govan and Granny called us up again. He was now at Shawlands Cross – where were we?

Kenny replied, 'Please note we were following a car and are now approaching Gorbals Cross!'

'Just remain there for a rendezvous,' said Granny.

Soon Granny called up that he was now at Gorbals Cross!

Kenny responded, 'We're up in Castlemilk!'

This continued for another few locations before the penny dropped with Granny that Kenny was yanking his chain and sending him all around the Southside of Glasgow.

Finally Granny said, 'Just cancel meantime and I'll see you back at the depot when you decide to come in for a break!'

Suffice to say, oh, no, he didn't!

Subtlety – the Best Way

...

On receiving a call about a complaint about some young boys annoying an elderly man, whereby the man had knocked one of the boys off his bicycle, my partner and I attended.

The mother of the boy making the complaint was a fat, disgustingly greasy-looking woman reeked of body odour and resembled a burst bin bag. (Good description, Morris.)

She was intent on telling us what she was going to do with this old man for causing her son to fall off his bike.

While she paused for breath, her impudent little four-teen-year-old brat of a son would interrupt and register his tuppenceworth about what he was also going to do with the old man.

Having spent some considerable time trying to convince them to agree to a police warning for the old man, we left and returned to our police car, which was double-parked alongside another vehicle with a young couple in the front seats.

As I got in our car, I was unaware that my driver's window was down and said to my colleague in a rather loud voice, 'See, instead of wasting our time and complaining about crap like that, she would be better employed tanning her son's bare arse for being so rude and disrespectful to the old man. She should also consider going on a crash diet to lose some of her excess weight, and maybe take a bath, the fat smelly cow!!'

My partner, seated beside me, just stared and raised his eyebrows at me.

Sensing there was something wrong, I started the engine and as I slowly turned around in the car, I was surprised to see the young couple in the car parked beside us staring at me with their mouths open.

Convinced they had heard my entire outburst, I looked straight across at them, smiled and said, 'Oh, hi there! Isn't it a lovely night for a drive?'

I then drove off, leaving them completely gobsmacked!

Stock Exchange News
. . .

I've just heard that apparently Marks & Spencer and Poundstretcher are to amalgamate their business resources.

The new stores will be known as Stretchmarks!

That's What She Said!
. . .

Whilst checking a statement taken by a young recruit regarding a road accident, I came across the following: 'As a result of the incident, I have a large bruise on my buttocks, bruises to my back and my face is sore. I'm also nine months pregnant'!

The Telephone Bill

· · ·

I attended a call to a house in the Castlemilk area regarding a report from a woman claiming to have had all her state benefit allowance books stolen.

I noted the various books referred to and obtained enough information to submit a crime report.

I went to the local post office to check if any of the books had been cashed there.

As luck would have it, one had been.

Could the teller remember whether it was a male or a female?

A description of what the person was wearing?

What time was it cashed?

These were just some of the questions you would ask.

The teller produced the signed stub from the allowance book.

I looked at the signature, which was clearly legible. 'Linda Johnstone?' I said, identifying the name.

'That's correct!' said the teller. 'She paid her telephone bill with it and I gave her the leftover change!'

The teller then produced the telephone bill stub belonging to her that she had paid.

On checking Linda Johnstone's address, she lived in the same tenement as the complainer. Too easy, I thought. And it was!

Apparently she had found the four books at the rear of the tenement building and kept the one book that was paying out enough money to cover her telephone bill.

She then posted the rest of the benefit allowance books

through the complainer's door so that she wouldn't be skint.

So she turned out to be a stupid thief but a fairly honest one.

I wonder if she had considered calling the police station with her reconnected telephone to report what she had done.

JFK
· · ·

Many police officers of a certain age remember where they were on that fateful day when President John F. Kennedy was assassinated.

Although such an event sticks in the memories of our older colleagues, it is sometimes a surprise to learn that half the world have only been born since then.

With this in mind, two police officers in the city centre were interviewing a not-too-bright female suspect.

When asked for her date of birth, she replied, 'The twenty-second of November 1963!'

The older cop, immediately recognising the significance of the date, said, 'I bet your mother remembers where she was when John F. Kennedy was shot dead.'

At which point the suspect protested, 'My mammy knows nuthin' about any shooting! She's no' like that! Who says she is? I'm her daughter and I have a right to know exactly what she's accused of and who grassed her up!'

Needless to say both cops just looked at each other, slightly bemused, and shook their heads.

Breakfast at Tiffany's

· · ·

It was the practice every morning on the early shift for the first cop in to make the toast and tea for the rest of the cops.

This applied mostly in the smaller, rural police offices.

One morning the shift had a new sergeant starting and he had been correctly given the nickname of 'Signal' – the tube with stripes!

He came in and sat down at the muster while I read out the detail to the shift, after which they all left to go out on their duties.

Afterwards, he called my partner and me into his office to say that in future we were to have our coffee and breakfast at home prior to coming to work, and not at work.

Disappointed by his pettiness, we decided to say nothing at this point and left his office.

Later the same day, we were engaged with an enquiry which was going to result in us having to work late.

The sergeant, dressed in his civilian jacket, was ready to go home and said he'd see us in the morning.

As he walked to the door, I remarked, 'We'll have your toast and tea ready for you arriving!'

Next morning, my partner and I arrived earlier than usual, armed with a surprise for Signal.

We both sat down at the office desk, each with a mug of tea and a brown paper bag in front of us, and waited for him to make an appearance.

Finally, as Signal opened the office door and entered, we

both produced bacon and egg rolls from our brown paper bags and took a bite out of them.

My partner then looked straight at Signal, standing there staring us, and said, 'I know what you're thinking, but this isn't our breakfast – it's actually last night's supper!!'

If I Had

. . .

My partner's father, Jim Dickson, would regularly come out with these wee Scottish sayings that were pure nonsense but kept youngsters well entertained. Here is one: 'Ificky iicky hadicky myicky gunicky, iicky wouldicky shooticky yonicky manicky onicky yonicky hillicky!'

'What does that mean, Jim?' I asked.

'Very simple, Harry,' he said. 'You just add "icky" to the end of each word. If I had a gun, I would shoot yon man on yon hill!'

Another I remember very clearly was when playing a game and we had to line up and say a rhyme to see who is 'het': 'Eely oaly, dug's toaly, you are out!'

Who the hell made them up, I ask you?

Answer the Phone

. . .

Along with my partner, I called at the home of David Dick to execute a warrant.

Having knocked on his door several times and received no response, I was about to leave when I noticed the house keys were in the inside door lock.

This prompted me to look through the letter box and on doing so I noticed a telephone on a table in the hall.

I left and went down to the lower landing of the tenement building, out of earshot, and contacted my radio controller at the station and asked him to look in the local telephone book for David Dick's home number.

Bingo! His number was listed, so I now requested the radio controller to call him.

I then went back upstairs to his door, lifted the letter box and waited.

Moments later, the phone began to ring in the hall.

It rang several times then, unable to resist a telephone ringing, David Dick appeared in the hallway from a nearby room, tip-toeing across the floor to answer it.

I watched him through the letter box as he slowly and deliberately tip-toed *Pink Panther* cartoon fashion towards the telephone.

Picking it up, he put it to his ear then answered in a soft whisper, 'Hello?'

To which the police radio controller on the other end replied, Hello, David Dick? It's the police here. Would you kindly go over and open the door to the officers waiting outside who wish to serve you with an apprehension warrant for your arrest?!'

He slowly turned around to see me peering at him through the letter box.

Having seen the funny side of it all, he burst out laughing and eventually opened the door to us.

Too Late

. . .

In the 1980s, I suffered a back injury which was to restrict my career and which remains with me to this day.

Many months were spent flat out on my back in hospital and in bed at home, when I eventually got out.

Having been a physically fit and active man, I found the simplest of tasks extremely difficult to do. Even walking unaided was a problem.

With all this inactivity comes depression and one day, whilst lying there flat out, waiting all day for a house visit from the doctor, I got extremely irate and fed up with the time it was taking so I called up the surgery and told the receptionist to inform the doctor not to bother making a house call: 'Mr Morris had just died!'

I'll tell you what – I got a fair old rollicking from the doctor but it worked, as he arrived within minutes of my replacing the handset!

Dusty Bin

· · ·

As I walked into the motorcycle canteen kitchen, Adam Cook was in the process of making himself a pot of tea.

His lunch box was lying open on the worktop, containing two sandwiches, an apple and a chocolate biscuit.

A shout rang out from another part of the office, 'Adam Cook, you're wanted on the telephone!'

I looked at him and said, 'Go get the telephone, Adam, and I'll make your tea for you.'

'Thanks, Harry!' he said, handing me the teapot.

While I made the tea, the door opened and in walked 'Dusty Bin', aptly named because he was one greedy fat bastard who ate non-stop.

He walked over and looked into Adam's lunch box.

'Whit have ye got for yer lunch, then, Harry?' ha asked, poking at the sandwiches with his fingers.

'Nothing much!' I replied, giving him the impression it was my lunch box. 'I had fish and chips earlier at the training school so I'm pretty much full up!'

'Are you going to eat these sandwiches, then?' he enquired.

'Definitely not!' I replied. 'I couldn't possibly eat them. It would just be greedy and totally out of order.'

'Do you mind if I help myself?' he pleaded.

'Do what you want, Dusty. I'm certainly not going to eat them!' I replied.

'Oh, thanks, Harry, you're a pal,' he replied, promptly helping himself to one of the sandwiches from the lunch box.

As he munched away on it, he said, 'Mmmm! They're tasty, Harry. Tell your missus she makes a mean sandwich!'

'I'll tell her, but my missus never made them,' I responded.

'Well, whoever made them, they're bloody good!' he replied.

I then remarked as I walked out of the kitchen, 'Yeah, they certainly look good, Dusty – wire in!'

'Can I have the other one?' he called out as I entered the rest room carrying Adam's pot of tea.

'Do what you like. I'm not going to eat them, that's for sure!' I replied as I sat down in the rest room, directly opposite the canteen entrance, closely followed by Dusty, armed with an apple in one hand and a half-eaten second sandwich in the other.

'There's no way you made these, Harry, so tell yer wife she makes a damn good sandwich!' Dusty reiterated.

'What, them?' I said. 'No way my missus made them. Unless she's having an affair that I don't know about!'

A few minutes later the door opened and Adam entered the rest room and, looking at us both, he said, 'Right! Where are my sandwiches? Where did you hide them?'

I immediately said, 'Well, Dusty? You were in the kitchen last!'

Dusty Bin gulped in horror, realising what I had done to him.

He then performed an excellent impersonation of an Ardrossan seagull as he swallowed his stolen Adam's apple whole!!

Match of the Day
· · ·

Dougie was a local who lived alone and suffered from severe bouts of manic depression.

Due to his mental condition, Dougie was prescribed medication which he had to take on a daily basis, and from time to time he was also hospitalised for lengthy periods.

During my nightshift duties, Dougie would regularly call at my station where I would offer him a sympathetic ear over a cup of tea and a cigarette.

However, one particular night he called in at the station and told me he was feeling like he wanted to hurt himself.

He had failed to take his medication for several days and I suggested he return to his house immediately and do so.

A short time later he returned, assuring me he had done as I requested, but he had in his possession his razor, a red Swiss army knife and a cigarette lighter, which he wanted me to keep safe while he was in this depressed state of mind.

I sat him down in the office and we had our usual blether with a cup of tea and several cigarettes until his medication kicked in and he appeared less agitated.

Apart from being a bit slow in his speech, Dougie could hold a serious and interesting conversation with you and he confirmed to me on many occasions, with his broad general knowledge, that he was an intelligent, educated and articulate man.

Considerably more calm and relaxed, he decided to go home and, as he was leaving, he asked me for a couple of cigarettes and some matches for a smoke later.

Without any hesitation, I duly obliged.

About an hour later, I was informed that Dougie had been arrested and subsequently sectioned under the Mental Health Act for setting fire to his house and trying to burn it down.

Fortunately no one was injured, but I often wondered if the fire was indeed deliberate or just an unfortunate accident!

However, it doesn't end there, because the sergeant who attended the call and apprehended Dougie called at my station and enquired as to how well I knew him.

Apparently Dougie had mentioned my name several times while he was being conveyed to the hospital.

I then related the story to the sergeant regarding Dougie's regular visits to the office and mentioned this latest one, whereby he had handed me his razor, knife and cigarette lighter.

I also informed him that, as Dougie had left, he had asked me for a few cigarettes and matches so he could have a smoke later.

Suddenly his facial expression changed and he said, 'You supplied him with matches?'

'Yes, Sergeant, I gave him a few matches. So are you trying to insinuate that I am to blame for the fire?' I asked.

'I'm not saying that at all, it's just that—'

I interrupted him and said, 'I suppose if he dies of lung cancer, you'll blame me for providing him with the cigarette that caused it? Get real!'

So, a bit of advice for you.

Don't give anybody a light and, even more ridiculous, don't hire a taxi to go anywhere, because if it is involved in a road accident where someone is injured or killed, and this sergeant attends it, he'll probably blame you for the taxi being at the accident spot!

Who, Me? No, You!

. . .

Following on the last story, I have been informed that all custody officers in the Strathclyde area have been given a checklist to assist them in recognising and dealing with prisoners who might be considered to be suffering mental illness.

Points are awarded on a scale, or points system, which includes such matters as:

regularly talking to themselves
overactive
continually feeling under threat
everything appears hopeless
expresses bizarre and outrageous ideas
unusually suspicious
always looking to pass the blame.

It has not gone unnoticed amongst the rank and file that several profiles of senior police officers currently employed in Strathclyde Police are being produced in accordance with this checklist!

Mermaid

• • •

I was involved, along with a well-known radio presenter, in a photo shoot for a local newspaper, to promote Road Safety Week.

We formed a good relationship and were swapping stories.

He was telling me about a woman who recently called the radio station in response to a music quiz and, during the live conversation, she informed him that she had a thirty-two-feet, five-berth cabin cruiser.

She then invited him out for a sail with her.

By this time he had formed the opinion she was hot and had an attractive, mysterious voice, so he accepted her open invitation to meet her.

However, she knew what he looked like but, apart from how she sounded on a telephone, he had no idea about her, but was more than a little intrigued.

He turned up at the agreed meeting place and after a few minutes his mysterious lady caller made her entrance.

Shockeroony! Horror!

'I'm a celebrity, get me out of here!' he cried aloud, but Ant and Dec were nowhere to be seen!

She may have sounded like a siren, however, in reality she resembled a sea horse!! She was humongous!!

He quickly made his excuses about a pre-arranged engagement that he had forgotten about and buggered off!!! Sharpish!!

A Pain in the Buttocks

• • •

Superintendent Alex Black, who was an absolute pain in the buttocks and a man who bullied everybody who was of a lesser rank to him just because he could, was regarded as a complete joke by other cops because it was believed that when a supervisor had to resort to bully-boy tactics to get things done, it was usually a clear indication that no one had any respect for them. True!

It was also regarded as a sign that they were not allowed to be the boss of their own house and were usually ruled by the wife – also probably true in his case.

One night he was the nightshift superintendent. This usually involved him being driven around the police stations in the division and signing the duty officer's journal in each office, confirming his visit.

At about one in the morning he arrived at my station, along with a young policewoman who had obviously drawn the short straw and been detailed to drive him about.

As I opened my duty journal and handed it over for him to sign, he took it from me and turned away.

With his back to me, I turned around to the bored policewoman with him and said, 'How did you manage to get lumbered with this detail?' and pointed over at him.

Her eyes widened, her jaw dropped and her face turned deep red.

At which point I then turned around quickly to face the superintendent.

As he looked straight at me, I tilted my head to one side and added, 'Sir?'

However, I'm positive to this day that he saw me in the office window!

For Fax Sake, Sir!

• • •

One day whilst working in the office, the station superintendent came through to me carrying a large package clearly marked 'Private and confidential'.

The package was sellotaped and sealed.

He then handed it over to me and said, 'I want you to fax this over to headquarters for me, Harry!'

I began to open it up, neatly tearing the sellotape, when the superintendent shouted at me, 'Stop! What the hell do you think you are doing? That clearly states "private and confidential" on there!'

I then had to explain to him that I had to remove the packaging to get to the papers in order to fax them.

He stood for a moment, deep in thought, then said, 'Oh! I didn't realise that. I thought you could just fax it all together as a parcel!'

As Homer Simpson would say – Doh!

I Don't Do That!

...

A colleague of mine, Jimmy Clark, and his wife Trish organised a house party for several members of the shift.

The booze was flowing and everything was going well.

I went to the toilet and on my return I had a whoopee cushion concealed in the rear of my trousers. As I sat back down on my chair, the cushion let out a rasper of a farting noise!

'Oops! Look out, Florida!' I said. 'But as Rabbie Burns would say, "Where e'er ye be, let yer wind gang free!"'

The assembled guests were all having a good laugh about it when suddenly Trisha, who was a very polite school teacher, interrupted proceedings and said, 'That's not one bit funny, Harry Morris. You're absolutely disgusting!'

This put a damper on the occasion as the laughing abruptly stopped.

For a moment there was complete silence and some of the party members felt slightly awkward at Tricia's outburst.

I said, 'Oh, come on, Tricia. Everybody does it at some point!'

Tricia, sitting on the floor, replied indignantly in her polite school teacher voice, 'That's where you are completely wrong, Harry Morris, because I most certainly don't!'

As she finished her sentence, she swung her legs up to cross them over, when – bbbbrrrrrpppppppp! What a rasper she let rip!!

Totally stunned and embarrassed by this untimely burst of flatulence, she said, 'Jimmy! Tell them I don't do that! Tell them, Jimmy! Tell them!'

However, try as she might, none of the guests were convinced, having just witnessed her untimely debut!

Childhood Poem

...

A favourite Glasgow poem I remember from my childhood about the Glesca polis is this:

> 'Murder! Murder!' polis, three stairs up
> The wummin up the next close hit me wi' a cup
> The cup wis aw broken, my heid wis aw cut
> 'Murder! Murder!' polis, three stairs up.

The Flasher

...

An elderly Jewish woman was making her way through the Gorbals late one night when suddenly a man appeared from a tenement close mouth and blocked her path.

He then opened up his raincoat and exposed himself.

Unruffled, she took a good look at him and remarked, 'You call that a lining?'

Play It Cool

...

In the late seventies, I was on mobile patrol with Tam Spencer and Jim Thompson. We were patrolling the Queenspark area of Glasgow, where a Republican march was taking place.

Tam, who also worked as a coalman, doing deliveries, carrying the heavy sacks up and down stairs on his days off, was about 5 foot 10 tall with hands like shovels and the thickest neck I have ever seen.

His neck was as broad as his shoulders and I kid you not.

The expression 'built like a brick shithouse' readily comes to mind.

Anyway, we received a call to attend the Royal Marines Territorial Army Halls in Maxwell Road regarding a complaint of a part-time marine having been seriously assaulted by a mob that had just entered a nearby pub.

We attended and took the necessary particulars for the crime report. One young soldier described the main instigator as a man in his early thirties, with short black hair and wearing a bright red V-neck jumper.

Tam, being the senior cop, said, 'Right, guys, here's how we play it. We're going into the lion's den here – this place is bursting at the seams with demonstrators and sympathisers, so let's play it cool. Firstly, when we go in, keep your back to the door and slide in along the wall, without causing too much fuss. Meanwhile, we survey the crowd and see if we can identify our man. If we see him, I'll quietly saunter over to him and invite him to come outside to talk. Whatever you do, do not take your baton out, OK? You mustn't show any sign of aggression.'

Having been briefed by Tam as to how we were going to deal with the situation, the three of us entered the pub.

Once we were inside the door, the atmosphere in the place could only be described as ugly.

Fortunately we spotted our suspect immediately, sitting at a table to our right, near the door, with about nine or ten others.

The table was covered in pints of beer with a large ashtray, about ten inches in diameter, on the centre of the table.

Tam leaned across the table and asked the suspect politely if he could speak with him outside.

'Are your eyes painted oan, big man? Can ye no' see I'm drinking and I've just got a round in for the table?' replied the suspect as his friends sitting around him laughed at his response.

He then lifted up a pint of beer and drank it down, then put the glass back on the table and joined in the laughter with his friends.

Big mistake! Not a man to mess with, Tam remained very calm and again politely asked the suspect to come outside so he could speak with him.

Having gained some bravado from his intake of alcohol, coupled with the support of his many friends around him, the suspect replied, 'Are you still here?' He continued, 'Either get a round in or get tae fuck oot ma face! I'm busy.'

As he turned away, he picked up another pint from the table and muttered, 'Arsehole!'

An even bigger mistake than the first!

Tam leaned over the table and wrapped his hand around the ned's wee hand that was holding the pint glass and began to squeeze it.

As the ned squirmed with the pain and the thought that the glass would smash in his hand, he put it back on the table.

At this, Tam grabbed hold of his collar and, with his other hand, picked up the ashtray and struck the ned across the head with it.

All hell broke loose as Tam then hauled the ned over the table with glasses of beer spilling everywhere and smashing on to the floor. Tam then dragged him past Jim and hauled him outside.

Jim and I followed them outside, but not before we stopped several objects with our bodies, such as bottles, glasses, ashtrays and other missiles thrown in our direction.

Once outside, we were able to draw our batons and put them through the door handles to detain the irate punters inside just long enough for more police support to arrive and quell the situation.

As for our gallus suspect, by the time we arrived at the station he had turned into a sober, quiet little mouse of a man with a thumping large lump on his head!

As for Tam, whenever I had the good fortune to work with him, I ignored all strategy being spouted by him and just played it by ear.

It was definitely a much safer option!

She's Dead? Ye're Joking!
...

Police attended a call to a house where the husband suspected his wife was dead.

The officers took one look at the wife lying in bed and called for the police casualty surgeon to attend.

The casualty surgeon arrived and, after examining the body, said to the husband, 'For goodness' sake, man, your wife has been dead for about a week! Did you not notice anything different?'

The husband shook his head.

'Not right away,' he replied. 'I mean, the sex was still the same, but I did notice the dishes were beginning to pile up in the sink!'

Road Accident Excuses
...

'The invisible car came out of nowhere. It then struck the side of my car and vanished.'

'I was thrown from my car as it left the road and was later found in a ditch by some stray cows who were lost.'

Get Off Lightly

. . .

A detective drank regularly in well-known former foot-baller Jim Baxter's pub at Paisley Road Toll, Glasgow.

One day a customer was talking to Jim and was telling him how, earlier that day, he had been stopped by the police and charged with speeding.

As this was his fourth time, he was resigned to the fact he would receive a hefty fine and a lengthy driving ban!

'Why don't you speak with Chas and see if he can do something for you? He's bound to know who to speak with,' advised Jim.

'Do you think so?' asked the customer.

'Well, it's definitely worth a try!' replied Slim Jim.

Later, Chas entered the pub and ordered up his usual!

'Let me get that for you, Chas!' said the customer.

'Cheers!' said Chas. 'Right, now, what are you after? Let's hear it,' he enquired from the punter.

The customer sat on the stool next to Chas and began explaining his plight.

After he finished, Chas said, 'It'll cost you twenty quid for me to speak with the procurator fiscal!'

'You're on,' replied the delighted customer and promptly handed over the £20.

Several weeks later, having been duly banned from driving, the customer called back at Jim Baxter's pub.

On seeing Chas sitting on a stool at the bar reading the newspaper, he went straight up to him and said, 'Ho, you! I gave you twenty quid to speak to the procurator fiscal and I still got done at the court!'

Quick as a flash, Chas asked him, 'What did you get?'

'I got fined a hundred quid and banned from driving for eighteen months,' he replied rather despondently.

'Well,' said Chas, 'just think what you would have got if I *hadn't* spoken to the fiscal!'

Weight and See

• • •

On duty at a football match one night, my colleague and I decided to visit a burger and coffee stall for something to eat.

We parked up our motorcycles and were walking towards the stall and removing our helmets when I heard Scoobie, the burger stall-holder, say in a loud voice, 'Quick, Isabel, hide yersel'! It's the Scottish Weight Watchers Squad and they're on a raid!'

I looked up to see this rather obese young girl assistant at the counter.

'Very funny!' she said, then proceeded to stuff the remains of a burger roll into her mouth!

Television Psychic
...

This is a story related to me by a TV licence inspector.

While working in a certain area, the detector vans had been spotted by the locals, who quickly spread the word about their presence.

One woman who did not possess a valid TV licence went to the local post office straight away and purchased one.

As it was, the TV detector van just happened to call into the street where she lived.

The woman was rushing out to her work and, on seeing the TV van, she knocked on the window and said, 'If you're going to number six, tell my man the TV licence is behind the big clock on the mantelpiece!'

With that she hurried on her way.

The TV inspector decided, since they were there, they might as well check it!

They knocked on the door and the husband, unaware of what had passed previously, answered it.

'Can I help you?' he asked.

The inspector identified himself and asked to see the TV licence.

The husband hesitantly said, 'I'm not sure where it is . . . but we do have one. It's just that the wife isn't in and she would have put it away.' Still stalling, he continued, 'Now let me think – where would she keep it?'

To which the TV Inspector said, 'I'll save you some time – it's behind the big clock on the mantelpiece!'

The husband went back in and, sure enough, there it was.

Returning to the front door with his TV licence in hand, he said, 'That's some bloody machine you have that can tell the exact position of where the licence is kept!!'

Alistair McGowan I'm Not!

• • •

A brilliant character I had the pleasure of working with in the early seventies, when we were part of the City of Glasgow Police, was John Reilly.

He was so laid-back and appeared to always be in control, even when he probably wasn't.

John also possessed a tremendously dry sense of humour.

Attending court one day to give evidence for the prosecution, John was called to the witness box to give his version of events, during which the procurator fiscal enquired of him, 'Constable Riley, can you please give the court your impression of the accused?'

John paused for a moment, before replying with total honesty, 'I'm terribly sorry, sir — I can tell you a joke, but I don't do impressions!'

Dick Bruce Elections

. . .

Dick Bruce was one of the senior cops on my shift when I worked at the Gorbals police station.

I found Dick to be a very competent officer with an excellent sense of humour, and as a result we had good fun working together, being of a similar mind.

It is true to say Dick was considered a rebel who would readily question decisions by supervisors if he felt they were incorrect, and due to this forthright manner, many officers felt they would be well-served if Dick was to stand for the position of Police Federation representative for the division at the forthcoming elections.

Now at this point I have to make it clear that the Police Federation is the equivalent in the police force to a works union and there was already an officer in this position, who had been there for several years.

However, as part of his campaign to make others aware of his intention to stand against the present representative, Dick asked me to come up with a slogan to circulate around the police stations to advertise his serious intentions.

I called at the Gorbals police station to meet with Dick and show him what I had come up with.

I produced a large piece of white A3 paper folded in half, on which was written in bold letters:

JOHN HAMILTON IS MAGIC!

Dick looked at me, unconvinced, until I unfolded the other half, which read:

AT THE NEXT FEDERATION ELECTIONS,
JUST WATCH HIM *DISAPPEAR*!
VOTE DICK BRUCE
NOW, HE *IS* MAGIC!

A wry smile broke out across Dick's face and he said, 'I love it, Harry boy!'

Needless to say the slogan went down well, not only with Dick but also with the other officers.

Whether it helped his cause or John's reign was at an end anyway, we'll never know, but suffice to say Dick was elected to serve as the divisional representative and, by all accounts, he never let anyone down.

High Court Trial

. . .

During a trial at the High Court in Glasgow, a witness was sworn in to give evidence.

He referred to himself as being a 'flying saucer', which he then explained to the jury and the beleaguered judge was Glasgow slang for a dosser or down-and-out with a serious drink problem!

'You mean you're an alcoholic, don't you?' said the advocate depute (prosecution).

'Well, you could say that!' he replied.

'I *am* saying that, Mr Barnes!' said the depute. 'Now, tell me, when was the last time you worked?'

'The last time I worked was the last time I was sober, sir!' he answered.

'And when was that?' asked the depute.

'I don't really remember, sir, but it was a while ago!' he replied.

'OK,' said the depute, changing tack. 'Tell me what you did on the day of the incident.'

'I bought a carry-oot wi' my giro money and went to the bench in the park to drink it.'

'And how long did you drink for?' enquired the depute.

The witness searched his brain for an answer, all the while pulling a silly face as he tried desperately to recall the moment.

Then his eyebrows raised and he proudly blurted out, in all sincerity, 'Until I fell off the park bench pished, sir!'

A short adjournment had to be called when the jury members fell off their seats laughing!

Oh, For a Neck Like a Giraffe

· · ·

The other night I called in at my local pub and, taking a seat on the stool at the bar, I ordered up a pint of heavy and a packet of crisps.

I sat there for several moments, eating crisps, drinking and reading my newspaper, when an older man entered the pub with a large Rottweiler.

As he sat down on the bar stool next to mine, he commanded his dog to lie down on the floor beside him and then ordered up a drink.

I was very impressed by the obedience of his dog in reacting immediately to his command.

As I was looking at this monster of a dog, it put its head between its hind legs and began to lick its testicles.

I jokingly remarked to the dog's owner, 'I would love to do that!'

To which he replied, 'If you give him one of your crisps, he might let you!'

Alfie and the Star Wars Game

· · ·

During one of his many heavy drinking binges, Alfie was accompanied by one of his booze buddies, wee John Scott, or Scotty as he was better known.

As they sat in a small booth in the pub, they noticed that their table was in fact an amusement arcade *Star Wars* game, which was plugged into the wall and required a pound coin to activate the game.

Alfie and Wee Scotty enjoyed several *Star Wars* battles during their boozing session, and when they were getting up to leave the pub Wee Scotty said, 'I'd love wan o' they game machines fur the hoose!'

'Whit fur?' enquired Alfie.

''Cause the telly is pish at night!' replied Wee Scotty.

'But where wid ye get wan frae?' asked Alfie.

'Nae idea, but . . . '

The penny dropped with both of them and they looked down at the game machine they had been playing with all afternoon.

'Whit dae ye think, Alfie?'

Alfie looked over at Wee Scotty and said, 'Quick! Grab an end o' it!'

They grabbed hold of the machine and, as they lifted it away, they pulled the wall plug from the socket.

Bold as brass, they walked out the door of the pub carrying the table, completely unnoticed by staff or patrons.

Unfortunately for our two opportunists, they only managed to walk a few hundred yards carrying their *Star*

Wars table when a passing police patrol car spotted them and stopped them in their tracks.

'Look out, Scotty boy. The Klingons are about to circle Uranus!' said Alfie.

Wee Scotty looked at the police officers approaching, then looked back at Alfie and said, 'What do you want to do, Alfie? Run?!'

Quick as a flash Alfie replied, 'Don't be stupid – the polis can travel at warp speed.'

'Well, what do you suggest, then?' asked Scotty.

Alfie paused for a moment, then blurted out, 'Beam me up!'

Both of them then fell about laughing as the two big policemen approached.

Try as Alfie and Scotty might to conjure up a believable excuse, the officers were having none of it and the pair were promptly arrested and, along with their booty, returned to the pub.

Fortunately for both of them, the landlord knew them both as regulars and with their state of intoxication he saw the funny side of their prank and did not press charges against them.

Alfie and Scotty were over the moon at this gesture.

However, it taught the landlord a lesson and from that night, all three gaming machines in the pub were chained to the floor to prevent a repetition of their act.

As a final piece to the story, you'll be 'star-struck' to know, the landlord just happened to be called James 'Jimmy' Kirk! (Retired captain of the *Enterprise* perhaps?)

Fortune's Told

...

My partner visited a clairvoyant recently to have her cards read.

After she was finished and was about to leave the clairvoyant's house, she opened the door with a bit too much gusto and the door swung open and struck a beautiful flower vase, knocking it to the floor, scattering the contents and breaking the vase.

My partner turned immediately to the clairvoyant and asked, 'Is that a sign of something, Betty?'

'Yes!' replied the clairvoyant. 'It's a sign that you're a clumsy bastard!'

Fire Sale

...

My brother-in-law Archie worked in the fire service and went around giving lectures to primary school children.

One day, after his lecture, he was asking questions, one being what do you do if your shirt catches fire?

One small boy's hand shot up in the air and he confidently said, 'Ask your mum to go to Asda and buy you another one!'

Biker Mad

. . .

Some time ago, whilst I was still a police motorcyclist, Billy Thomson and I were partnered together.

Billy had just completed his Advanced Motorcycling course and was eagerly showing off.

We had stopped a young guy riding a Vespa scooter and were talking to him when Billy suggested he would love to try his Vespa to experience the difference between a scooter and a motorcycle.

The young guy agreed to his request and Billy sat on the scooter, started up the engine and decided to give it full throttle.

As he released the clutch, the scooter shot forwards and Billy shot backwards off the seat and, still hanging on to the handlebars, he was dragged embarrassingly along the road, coming to an abrupt halt when he collided with a garden hedge!

Clarky in Pet Shop

· · ·

My long-time friend and former police colleague Jimmy Clark drove up from his home in Darvel, Ayrshire, one evening to attend, along with myself, the retirement doo of one of our former police colleagues.

Deciding not to drive to it, we left together in a taxi, expecting the worst — that we were going to end up totally pissed!

During the evening, Jimmy had a great time revelling in the infamous Glesca patter, which was flowing freely.

Patter that he no longer heard, having left Glasgow several years before to continue his career in Ayrshire.

At the end of the evening, I helped carry Jimmy (although to this day he maintains it was he who helped carry me) into the taxi for the journey home.

After several 'one more for the road' whiskies, Jimmy, who was staying the night at my house, retired to his bed.

The next morning I decided to spare Jimmy from tasting my home cooking and drove him to the local supermarket restaurant for a big breakfast of sausage, bacon, black pudding, egg, potato scone, beans, tomato and mushroom, served with orange juice and a mug of hot tea to wash it all down.

Afterwards, we went to a giant pet store to get some tasty treats for my dog.

Whilst waiting in line at the checkout to pay for my goods, I observed a small man in the next aisle struggling to carry a rectangular glass aquarium through the narrow checkout.

A man immediately in front of me in the queue, watching the struggling male and obviously recognising him, called over, 'Is that you under that big tank, Tam?'

'It is that, George!' replied the man, huffing and puffing uncontrollably.

'Have you got fish, then?' enquired George.

'Naw! No' fish, George – lizards!' he replied, still struggling to keep hold of his aquarium.

'Lizards!' George muttered, then paused for a moment before repeating, 'Lizards?'

'Aye, lizards!' confirmed Tam.

To which George blurted out, 'Big bastards, eh?'

At this off-the-cuff Glaswegian remark, Jimmy Clark burst out laughing, quickly followed by the rest of the customers in the vicinity.

To Jimmy, this was the priceless Glasgow talk which he sorely missed and which he only experienced now and again during the odd excursion up to Glasgow.

The Superintendent's New Car

. . .

The regular driver for chauffeuring the nightshift superintendent around the divisions had called the office to report he was going to be late and asked if it would be possible for his new car to be delivered to him in order to save time.

Now, I have to explain that the nightshift superintendent's car was a brand new, deep blue Ford Granada Ghia, automatic, with all the extras required, making it an absolute luxury to drive.

During the muster, when the shift are detailed their duties, O'Reilly and I were instructed to deliver the aforesaid car to the duty driver's house, followed by the words, '*Remember it's an automatic, so make sure you drive it carefully and don't let anything happen to it!*'

As we walked through the office to collect the car keys, O'Reilly brushed me aside and grabbed the keys for the Granada.

Turning to me, he said, 'Race you!' then ran off outside to the motor pool garage to collect the car.

By the time I reached the garage entrance, O'Reilly was driving out in the flash Granada Ghia.

As he passed within a whisker of me, he lowered the electric window, gave a wave like the Queen does and said, 'If you're no' fast, you're last!'

He then drove out the garage and shouted at me, 'Catch me if you can!' before laughing uncontrollably and driving off at speed, thus leaving me to carry out visual and mechanical checks to my patrol car before I could drive off after him, several minutes later.

I drove on to the motorway and after a short time I accessed the road to Linwood, where I spotted O'Reilly along the road, standing in the middle of the carriageway, waving his arms frantically, signalling for me to stop.

As I approached, I could see the reason for his panic as flames and smoke bellowed from the front of the superintendent's car.

'Quick!' shouted O'Reilly. 'Give me your fire extinguisher!'

Armed with the extinguisher, O'Reilly went to the front of the car to try and control the fire in the engine compartment, while I called for the services of the fire brigade.

After what must have seemed like an eternity for O'Reilly as the fire brigade checked that the fire was thoroughly extinguished and saturated it with half the water supply for the Paisley area, the nightshift superintendent's luxury car was whisked away by tow truck to the Helen Street police garage to ascertain the cause.

As he sat in the passenger seat of my patrol car, pondering what to tell the boss, I couldn't resist asking him, 'So tell me, how does it handle at speed, then?'

This prompted him to look me straight in the eye and utter the immortal and well-used, 'Bastard!'

Back at the garage, it only took the duty sergeant minutes to discover that O'Reilly had not changed the automatic lever from 'Drive 1' to 'Drive' while driving the car 70mph, thereby causing the engine to blow up and burst into flames.

Final diagnosis: a complete new engine and respray required for the nightshift superintendent's car and several months of indoor gatehouse duties for O'Reilly, driving a brand new office desk!

Irish Humour
• • •

A young Irish girl went home and told her parents, 'I'm pregnant!'

Her dad said, 'Are you sure it's yours?'

Nine months later she gave birth to six piglets.

Her father is now looking for the swine that did it!

Big Joe's Party

• • •

Big Joe Strong and I had been performing a stake-out in a local pub, following information about drugs being dealt inside by a relatively well-known ned.

As part of the sting we were on, we both had to indulge in a small alcoholic libation so as not to look out of place.

Big Joe, for his part, talked non-stop about a new patio he was having built at the rear of his house, with the new patio doors already installed.

Several drinks later, with no apparent drug-deal action taking place, we were instructed to stand down.

As we returned to our office to end our duty for the day, we learned that one of our senior police colleagues (some old bugger that had hidden away in an office for the last twenty-five years and had a sell-by date stamped on his arse) was celebrating his forthcoming retirement from the force in the canteen with other shift members.

Having had a taste of alcohol and whetted our thirst, it was suggested we should show our faces at the retirement celebrations and sample a few free drinks.

This we did, mingling with the other officers, exchanging funny stories and making enquiries into whom the bloke retiring was and where he worked.

At the end of the evening, big Joe invited three of us back to his house in Eaglesham – 'Hutch', wee Brian and myself – with the guarantee of continuing our drinking session.

Wee Brian, the youngest of us, had not been drinking and volunteered to drive us up to Joe's house, via his own house where he would collect a bottle of vodka to add to our carry-out.

Now, big Joe was married to a big ex-policewoman called Maggie and, prior to arrival at his house, I just had to get him to confirm that she was aware of our late-night appearance in her home and was in full agreement.

This confirmed, we duly arrived at the house.

Once inside, the party commenced with the drink flowing freely.

To start with, the music was kept to a tolerable level, then, as we relaxed with more drink, it gradually rose by several decibels.

I decided to spare the neighbours and closed the curtains across the open patio doors. They would still hear us, but at least they wouldn't have to see our crazy antics.

Within minutes, big Joe had the wedding-present canteen of cutlery out and we were all issued with the spoons to hit off our knees, hands or any other part of our anatomy that we could make a noise from.

Hutch got completely carried away with the drink. One minute he was dancing around the lounge like one of the crazy flower-power hippies from the sixties, with a bunch of plastic flowers in his mouth, and the next minute he had disappeared completely from view.

Now, I wasn't that drunk that I didn't notice, so being a polis I decided to investigate his disappearing act! As it was, he had danced around in circles that much he had become dizzy and went to lean against the drawn curtains, not realising that the new patio doors behind them were open, and he had fallen straight through the opening and was now lying in a crumpled heap on the concrete base of big Joe's unfinished patio.

'What are you doing down there, Hutch?' I enquired. 'Don't tell me – you're trying to break a bar of toffee in your back pocket!'

'Break a bar of toffee? I think I've broken my arse!' replied Hutch, putting his hand round to examine. 'It feels all funny!' he said.

As I helped Hutch up on to his feet, I realised he had broken his mobile phone in the back pocket of his trousers.

'Not at all, you're OK!' I said (lying through my teeth).

We got back inside, just in time to see a large shadow descend over us like a total eclipse.

It was big Maggie!

At three in the morning, awakened from her beauty sleep, she was not a pretty sight to behold. Suffice to say she frightened the life out of me.

'Right, ya shower o' noisy bastards!' she bellowed.

'What's up, sweetheart?' enquired a sheepish big Joe.

'Don't you "sweetheart" me!' she shouted. 'Get you and Pan's People tae fuck oot my living room and go annoy some other poor bastard!'

'But, sweetheart, I've said they can stay!' big Joe tried to reason with her.

Big Maggie interrupted him. 'Stay? You'll be lucky if Ah let *you* stay! Now get tae fuck out before I batter the lot of you!'

No sooner said than done – we were off and running down the road like schoolboys, laughing hysterically and checking behind us every now and again in case big Maggie was following us.

Frankie the Make-Up Artist

• • •

A few years ago I was approached by a traditional Scottish/Irish folk band and asked to manage them.

This entailed organising proper rehearsals, raising their profile and performing all administration duties.

Several months into the job, I arranged a twenty-one-day tour to Moscow.

This was an exciting prospect, having never visited the country before, but I was pleasantly surprised by the fantastic reception we received, and the agent organising our concerts was very able.

The members of the band were all excited and up for it as we looked forward to our first performance.

Frankie was the percussionist in the band and very much in love with himself and his appearance. With this in mind, he purchased a long piece of braided hair and would attach it under his own thinning, short hair to hang down and make him look a cool dude.

Not finished there, he would wear a feileadh-mhor, the long tartan kilt material you wrap artistically around you, with leather straps wrapped around both wrists and legs.

Finally, to complete the image, Frankie decided to give himself the St Tropez look with a cheap bottle of false tan he had acquired from the Barras market, advertised by the salesman as, 'The genuine article, cost £49.99 in the shops, selling today for only £3 a bottle or two for a fiver!'

This, to Frankie, who was a total attention-seeker, would definitely make him stand out from the other members of the band on stage, so he had purchased the bargain two bottles.

The opening concert duly arrived and the audience was buzzing with expectation, having seen the band interviewed on Moscow television.

'Where's Frank?' I enquired from the other band members in the dressing room.

'He's just in the toilet, boss!' replied Hamish. 'Probably a bit of first-night nerves, but he'll be OK!'

As I assembled the others and wished them all the best for a good concert, I could hear our Russian promoter going through his build-up announcement, then we were on.

As the others began to file past on to the stage to rapturous applause from our Russian audience, I shouted on Frankie.

Click! The toilet door opened and out came Frankie, looking like Michael Jackson in reverse.

He had gone in white and come out brown!

With no time to say anything, I ushered him on to the stage.

I watched the reaction of the others as he made his appearance, but like true professionals they didn't make a big deal of it.

However, his obvious change in appearance prompted the Russian promoter to enquire of me, 'Harry, what is wrong with Frankie? His colour?'

I did my best to play it down.

'Oh, it's just an old army ritual, Vitaly. He used to be in the Black Watch and out of respect he still likes to put on some camouflage now and again!'

Vitaly looked at me totally unconvinced and said, 'The Black Watch? Come off it, Harry – he looks more like one of the Four Tops than a Celtic folk singer!'

'Aye, all right, Vitaly,' I admitted. 'He's overdosed on his cheap St Tropez false tan fluid!'

That said, we both had a laugh and then went out front to take our seats and enjoy the performance.

Everything was going fine and the Russian audience were extremely appreciative of the music being performed for them.

Then disaster struck for Frankie, who was posing like a fanny and trying to look ultra-cool.

Well, it would have been OK if he *had* stayed cool, but due to the sweat worked up with the performance coupled by the intense heat from the stage lights, poor Frankie began to perspire profusely and it wasn't too long before his St Tropez false tan was running off his face and leaving obvious white stripes.

There was also another very noticeable mistake made by Frankie.

You see, Frankie had decided to give his legs the same treatment, but had rubbed the cream on to the front of his legs, forgetting that you really should rub it on the back of your legs as well.

As a result, when he turned his back to the audience, his legs and neck were pure white, which was blatantly obvious to everyone in the audience, bar one blind man.

And as if that wasn't enough to contend with, Frankie had also put mascara on his eyes, eye brows and even used it to draw on his very fashionable pointed sideburns à la Midge Ure!

'Mascara' should have been spelt 'massacre' – it was a disaster!

Poor Frankie – all his effort to try and look the coolest dude on stage had backfired to disastrous effect, and by the end of the performance, what with continually wiping the sweat from his face, he resembled a cross between Alice Cooper and Ozzy Osbourne, with his black mascara smudged and running everywhere.

The ideal look if you want to haunt a house, but not recommended for a Celtic folk band performing Scottish and Irish music on stage in Moscow.

However, all was not lost as the band, the audience, the promoter and myself had a right good laugh at his expense.

For his bit, Frankie mixed with the younger members of the adoring Russian audience, totally unaware of his streaky-bacon look until Hamish couldn't resist any longer and took great pleasure in holding up a mirror and pointing it out to him.

For the first time in his life, Frankie decided to make a hasty retreat and run away from female company, with no threat of an irate husband or jealous boyfriend in sight – for a change!

Needless to say he was never allowed to forget it and was regularly reminded of it during performances, when I would relate the story to our future audiences, promoting hilarious bouts of laughter.

The Memo!

...

The following is a tongue-in-cheek memo dated 3 July 1983, from Inspector Ian Downie to the motorcycle sergeants, with regards to a surplus Portakabin from Chester Street being delivered to the Traffic Department office at Meiklewood Road for the use of the motorcycle section.

PORTAKABIN FOR MOTOR CYCLE SECTION

On the arrival of the Portakabin this morning from Chester Street, it was apparent that it would require to be thoroughly cleaned before it is fit for use, even by your lot in the motorcycle section.

Consequently, I would suggest that Constable Harrison be detailed to sweep it out and wash down the walls and windows.

Both the toilets are also boggin' and I suggest Harry Morris be detailed to clean them as he is always in the shit anyway.

It is intended to have a telephone installed, not in the toilets but in the main area, to stop Sgt Brydon moaning about the boys using his telephone all day.

Electricity will also be connected whenever that 'bright spark' Bob Hunter can fit it in.

Plumbing work will be undertaken by Constable Alex Irvine and his boy Peter Kilpatrick as they are the most experienced in this field — just don't ask them to repair a motorcycle.

If the outside requires cleaning then an officer with permanent waterproof leggings should be detailed, therefore Constable Harry Menzies would be an ideal choice because he never takes them off.

If the top of the roof is dirty then Sgt Donald McArthur should be selected to clean same, as we do not have a ladder to reach up to it.

Once it is operational, the following safety precautions MUST be observed.

Due to the fact that both toilet cubicles are situated at the same end of the Portakabin, the following officers must not be allowed to use the toilets at the same time (not the same cubicle but cubicles at the same time – two into one doesn't go): *PC Kenny Ferguson, PC Eddie Oliver* and *PC Jim McGurk*.

In the event of any combination of the above officers being in the 'thunder-boxes' at any one time, there is a grave possibility that the Portakabin will tilt up on its end.

PS. Don't show this to a certain Harry Morris or it'll probably end up in his Motorcycle Magazine.

My Appreciation

· · ·

The author would like to thank you for buying this book and hopes that you had as much fun reading it as he had writing and compiling it.

The author would also like to thank the many police colleagues/characters who made it possible to write about all this but impossible to tell the real truth.

The author would also like to add that most of the names have been changed to protect the guilty and most of the stories have been exaggerated!

The Harry the Polis cartoons were created and written by Harry Morris and illustrated by Derek Seal.

Harry Morris, who appears courtesy of his parents, is available as an after dinner speaker for functions and can be contacted by email at:

harry.morris51@virgin.net.

Or by post:

PO BOX 7031, GLASGOW, G44 3YN. SCOTLAND.